WOMEN EMPOWERMENT

A Key to Development

WOMEN EMPOWERMENT

A Key to Development

Dr. Raj Kumar

Neha Publishers & Distributors
Delhi - 110002

Neha Publishers & Distributers
4832/24, Prahlad Gali, S-204, Ansari Road,
Darya Ganj, New Delhi - 110002
Tel. : 23278261, 43570976
E-mail : gauravbookcentre@gmail.com
Website : www.gauravbookcentre.com

Ist Edition, 2011

ISBN : 978-93-80318-08-0

Prise : ₹895/-

Laser Typesetting by : Tamalika Computers, Delhi

Printed at : Balaji Offset, Delhi-32

PRINTED IN INDIA

Published by Mrs. S. Chaudhary for Neha Publisher & Distributor, Delhi-110002

Contents

Preface 7

1. Women's Empowerment and Emancipation 9
2. Gender Equality and Women's Empowerment 26
3. Women Empowerment: A Key to Development 69
4. Women's Empowerment for Sustainable Agriculture Development 91
5. Historical Profile of Women in India 107
6. Indicators of Women's Empowerment in India 123
7. Women Empowerment in India - Milestones & Challenges 142
8. Women Empowerment and Development 173

Appendix: Women in Power and Decision-Making 190

Preface

Empowerment of women has multiple benefits. United Nations Report titled the state of world population 1992, proclaimed that there can be no sustainable development without development for women, because it is women who contribute more for the development of children and their full, equal and benificial involvement in decision-making process can alone lead to sustaible development.

This book, therefore, attempts to provide to the readers, best and inssorative sources on different aspects of women empowerment. While selecting the material for this volume care has been taken to include essays from prominent authorities on the subject to suit the needs of scholars, students and even general readers.

We respectifully acknowledge the contribution of authorities on the subject and librarians and their staff members.

Last but not the least, my publisher deserves patronage of the readers, for publishing this useful material for further studies and indepth analysis of the subject of profound importance.

Out readers satisfaction with the book will be our best rewards.

1

Women's Empowerment and Emancipation

What is Women's Empowerment?

We all know that the Constitution of India has conferred equal rights on women and men. We are also aware of the fact that discrimination on the grounds of gender is prohibited by the Constitution. For the last 175 years, several laws have been passed to liberate women from the clutches of customs and practices which have been oppressing them for centuries. Yet, we see that many women face discrimination from birth to death. Laws are no doubt very important to emancipate women from oppression, but it is equally important to create an environment in which equality can be enjoyed equally by all women. It is the creation of this environment which is the goal of empowerment.

Who is an Empowered Woman?

An empowered women is one who:

- Has the freedom to make choices and take decisions in matters relating to her life as well as society at large.
- Is not a victim of violence either in her family or any other social institutional setting.
- Can live her life in such a way that her self-respect and dignity are protected.

- Has equal access (equal chance) to opportunities in all spheres of activity.
- Is in a position to make use of the laws formulated for safeguarding her honour and rights.

Mere provision of opportunities for women is not enough. They must have the freedom to make use of these opportunities. Let me give you an example. Six-year-old Leena lives in a village. She wants to go to the village primary school like her friends, but her family want to send her to work as a domestic help in the neighbouring city. Being a citizen of India, Leena has as much right as any other girl in the country to go to school, but due to poverty and family pressure she is forced to give up her ambition. Leena is not empowered to make use of her rights. So empowerment is a condition when women/girls have the freedom to enjoy a right in practice and not just in theory.

Why should women be empowered?

Women constitute nearly half of India's population. So, unless an environment is created in which women are able to enjoy all their rights and live without fears or restrictions, India cannot progress. When women are empowered, an emancipated and enlightened (*liberal / open-minded*) society is created. Even today a large number of women are forced to confine (*limit / narrow*) their lives within the four walls of their homes. Though there are no legal hurdles to their emancipation, social and cultural restrictions have prevented them from using opportunities for their development.

Human history is full of examples of women who have taken leadership positions and guided the destinies of their nations. Women have made a significant contribution for the survival and sustenance of communities. Women's work both in the domestic sphere and outside has helped the society move ahead. Hence women need to be empowered both in their personal lives and as members of society. We can quote here the UNFPA (*United Nations Fund for*

Population Activities) Report titled the State of World Population 1992, which said that there can be no sustainable development without development for women, because it is women who contribute more for the development of children. Empowerment of women has multiple benefits not only for the environment but for humanity as well. Ensuring sustainable development requires women's empowerment and their full, equal and beneficial involvement in decision-making process related to sustainable development. It also requires their participation as planners, managers, scientists and technical advisors in all fields.

When women are empowered, they empower society. They have concerns not only for their families but also for the entire community. When women are given access to resources they generally spend it on the well being of larger numbers, be it their family or neighbourhood. The example given below will make it clear.

Empowered women create an empowered society

The elderly women of the village called *Shantigrame* started a Day Care Centre for small children. They pooled their small savings and rented a small place to start this Centre. An NGO working in the village also gave them some financial support. There were a number of young girls in this village who were forced to drop out of school because they had to take care of their younger siblings. When the day care centre was started, the infants and very young children were being left there and the young girls went back to school. The parents of the children gave a small token amount to the elderly women who ran the day-care centre, and this small earning gave them resources to improve their own lives. School drop-out numbers reduced considerably and in course of one year, life in the village changed. During the next four years, a high school and a junior college were also started in Shantigrama and every girl in the village attended school or college, as the case may be. Do you now see, how a few women who were empowered and encouraged to look for means of supporting themselves, also empowered other women and girls in their village.

It is thus necessary to empower women. An empowered woman creates a better home and a better society. If she herself is in bondage, how can she help others? So a woman must have the strength and support to lead her life in a free and just atmosphere.

Emancipation

The term emancipation refers to a condition of release from any form of oppression or bondage (*oppression / control*). The removal of hurdles or constraints for achievement of one's goals in life can also be called emancipation. Emancipation can be achieved through legal or social action. Many a time action leads to legal action.

Struggles for the Emancipation of Women in India - The Beginnings

On the eve of British conquest of India, the position of women was very humiliating. Social evils such as female infanticide, *sati*, child marriage, restrictions on female education, polygyny and ban on widow marriage flourished. In the name of religion, women were kept away from all efforts to seek empowerment. For more than two hundred years after they set foot in India, the British did not interfere with the religious and social life of the people they governed because of their policy of non-interference. But as their position in India was strengthened (*became strong*), the British started responding positively to the efforts of enlightened Indian social reformers who had launched a struggle to emancipate women from the clutches of evil social practices and customs. The period between 1829 and 1947 saw the enactment of many laws, which aimed at emancipating women from the clutches of oppressive social customs. Indian social reformers had to work against heavy odds and stiff social opposition.

A change-resistant (*opposing change*) society did not accept the ban on Sati or the legal sanction for widow marriage so very easily. Though *sati* was legally banned in 1829, incidents of *sati* continued and even as late as 2002 cases of *sati* were still being reported. If an inhuman practice like *sati* could exist even in the 21st century, when so much progress has been made in the fields of science and technology, you can well imagine how difficult it must have been to fight for women's emancipation over one hundred and seventy years ago.

Lifting the ban on widow remarriage was another major step in the struggle for the emancipation of women. While the ban on *sati* was somewhat effective, the Widow Remarriage Act of 1856 could not be effectively implemented because of social opposition. But the freedom, which the law gave widow to marry was definitely an achievement in the struggle for women's emancipation. With a ban imposed on *sati* and the ban on widow marriage removed, an environment for liberating women was created.

One of the greatest obstacles to women's emancipation was child marriage. The enactment of the child Marriage Restrain Act in 1929 prescribed the minimum age at marriage for a girl as 14 and a male as 18 years. Though 14 years is by no means the right age for a girl to be married, this Act at least took the bold step to put an end to the evil custom of infant marriages. When girl children did not have to be married off an an early age, they could go to school which is a very effective instrument of emancipation. The 1929 Act was the single most significant piece of legislation that sought to emancipate women in the pre-independence era.

Most of the social reformers of the 19th century strongly advocated women's education, for they saw education as the single most important tool for liberating women. The opening of schools, especially meant for girls was a major step in efforts at emancipating women. When women got an opportunity to move out of their homes and also an exposure to the world at large, they were lifted out of ignorance. Though conservative parents did not really accept the idea of sending their daughters to school easily, the fact that efforts began to be made for providing education to girls, was itself a major step in the direction of women's emancipation.

The social reform movements of the 19th century, the efforts made in the early part of the 20th century and also the 19th century women's movement in Europe and North America laid the foundation for the emergence of a strong women's movement in India. The freedom struggle brought many women out of their homes and the newfound awakening created the right atmosphere for fighting for their rights. Liberation from colonial rule and freedom from oppressive social customs were the twin goals of the struggles for women's emancipation. Initially the movement for women's equally was spearheaded by men, but during the later years the leadership passed on to women. Between 1880 and 1930, a number of women's organizations sprang up all over the country. By the time India won her freedom, the stage was set for launching the women's movement on a firm footing.

What is the women's movement?

Women's movement refers to the struggles launched by individuals and groups for liberating women from the clutches (control) of social evils and also for establishing equality between men and women. Women's movement is also referred to as the Women's Liberation Movement. The ideology of the women's movement is that women have equal rights and opportunities available in society. Women's movement believes in activism or action directed at ensuring that women get their rightful place in society. The women's movement fights against oppression of women in all social institutions. It also acts as a pressure group (a group whose voices and actions influence public policy and public opinion) and urges the state to enact laws, which give women their due share in the economic and political affairs of the country. The ultimate goal of the women's movement is to create an environment in which women's self-dignity is safeguarded both in private and public sphere.

Women's Empowerment Efforts in Independent India

The ongoing efforts to empower the women of India are made by the state, voluntary organizations and women's groups. Voluntary women's groups are also known as autonomous women's groups. The common element in efforts being made both by the state and autonomous women's groups is the recognition of the fact that there is gender discrimination in our society and that special emphasis must be placed on eliminating it. If the Constitutional guarantee of equal opportunities and prohibition of discrimination has to become a reality (*put into practice*), there has to be a constant effort to identify and remove gender inequalities. The approaches and strategies of the state and voluntary efforts, however, are different. So, it is important to study the two separately. Let us first see what the state has done to empower women.

State Initiatives for Women's Empowerment

Law has been viewed as a powerful instrument of social change. The process of emancipating women from the clutches of oppressive social customs started even before India became independent. Since 1829, when the Sati prohibition Act was passed, a number of laws have been passed to remove the legal hurdles to women's empowerment. We have also seen that amendments have been brought to many of the existing laws in order to make them stronger and more stringent. But law alone cannot bring about a change in the position of women. Constant and special efforts have to be made to improve their standards of living. This was mainly sought to be done through the Five Year Plans.

The Five Year Plans

The planning process was started in India in 1951 with the primary objective of removing the hurdles for emancipation for all section of India's population. Each Five-Year plan had identified certain priority areas, and improving women's status was only one aspect of the plan programmes. We are now seeing the X Plan in operation and in order to understand what each Plan has done for women, let us go through the approaches and achievements of the different Five Year Plans.

> **From Welfare to Development to Empowerment**
> Over the years the planning strategies (line of action) for women have shifted from Welfare to Development and to Empowerment. It is this shift which needs to be critically examined if we wish to understand the role of the state in women's empowerment.

First to Fifth Five Year Plans

The approach of the First Five Year Plan (1951-56) was to provide adequate services to promote the welfare of women so as to enable them to play their legitimate role in family and community. Here, the emphasis was on welfare and hence women were treated as mere recipients of incentives, which the state chose to give. The Plan called for setting up of special organizations both at the central and state levels for promoting the welfare of women. The Central Social Welfare Board was set up in 1953. It has its branches in the states. These boards have been supporting and conducting a number of programmes, mainly with a thrust on (*with and emphasis on*) economic advancement.

The approach of the Second, Third, Fourth and Fifth Five Year Plan was in no way different from that of the First Five Year Plan. The welfare approach still guided policies and programmes, which were launched for women's development. Only two special schemes were introduced during this period. These were, the condensed Course of Education and Women and Socio-Economic Programme introduced during the second Plan (1956-61) and Working

Girls Hostels and Short Stay Homes introduced during the Fourth Plan (1969-74).

Towards Equality – A Report, which Actually Set the Government and Voluntary Groups Thinking

In the year 1974, the Committee on the Status of Women in India submitted a report, which was aptly titled *Towards Equality*. This Report, paved the way for serious thinking on the status of women in different social institutions in India, because it showed that women were far behind men in enjoying the equal rights conferred on them by the Constitution. This Report led to a debate in the Parliament and showed the failure of the welfare approach, which treated women as recipients of benefits and not as equal partners in the development efforts.

The new consciousness that emerged after the publication of *Towards Equality* has to the setting up of the Women's Welfare and development Bureau in 1976 under the Ministry of Social Welfare. Four separate working groups on employment of Women, Adult Education Programmes for Women, Women in Agriculture and Rural Development were also set up to work on strategies for action.

Sixth Five Year Plan: The Shift from Welfare to Development

From the *Sixth Plan (1980-85)* onwards, a marked shift took place from the Welfare to a Development approach. How are the two different? While the welfare approach treated women as beneficiaries or receipents of benefits, the development approach recognized women as participants in development and not as development targets. It was not enough to introduce a few women specific scheme, but there was need to strive for an all round development of women. Look at the example given below:

1. A women in the village was given tailoring lessons under one of the government schemes. But, she had no other means of economic support to buy either a sewing

machine or other accessories (*items*) needed to open a small tailoring business. So her training was going waste. She was treated as a target of a welfare programme and afterwards nobody asked her what she really wanted. This is an example of the welfare approach with fixed targets.

2. Before sanctioning women's development programme in a village, a meeting of the women who were residents of the village was called. They were asked to name a few programmes which they thought would be helpful to them to better their economic status. they were also asked to give suggestions as to how best these programmes could be implemented. Since the women identified the setting up of a milk-cooperative and basked weaving as their priorities, the development agency started a milk cooperative and provided the initial funding. Training in basket weaving, specially keeping the market needs in view was also given. In this case women were not treated simply as beneficiaries or receivers of a welfare programme, but they were consulted about their choice of a programme and also involved in managing the programme. This is an example of the development approach.

Towards the end of the Sixth Five Year Plan i.e., in 1985, the Department of Women and Child Development was set up as part of the Ministry of Human Resource Development. This Department was created to function as a central agency to formulate and implement plans, policies and programmes for the development of women and children.

The Seventh Five Year Plan

The Seventh Five Year Plan (1985-1990) laid emphasis on generation (*creation*) of employment opportunities for women. Two new schemes – Support to Training and Employment (STEP) and Awareness Generation Programme for Rural and poor Women (AGP) were introduced. Three important Reports, which were to serve as useful guidelines for future development programmes of the government, were also released during the Seventh Plan period. These were:

- Shrama Shakti (Report of the National Commission on Self-Employed Women and Women in the Informal Sector).
- National Perspective Plan on Women (1988-2000).
- SAARC Guide Book on Women in Development.

The Decade 1990-2000 was declared as the SAARC Decade of the Girl Child and as part of this event, programmes laying special thrust on (*giving special importance to the*) the overall development of girl children were launched.

Landmarks (highlights) of the Eighth Plan

The Eight Plan (1990-95) period saw the creation of two major organizations, one aimed at social empowerment and the other at economic development of women. The National Commission on Women is a statutory body constituted under the National Commission for Women Act 1990. Its main duties are the protection of the interest of women by safeguarding their rights. The Rashtriya Mahila Kosh was set up in 1993 mainly to facilitate credit support and micro-finance to poor women.

The Eight Plan Period also saw a revolutionary amendment to the Constitution of India, which provided for the reservation of one-third of the seats in Panchayatiraj institutions and urban local self-governing bodies such as municipalities and corporations to women. The 73rd and 74th Constitutional amendments, which made this reservation possible, have gone down in the history of women's empowerment in India as a 'democratic revolution'. Today, there are more than 40,000 women in local governing bodies across the country, a phenomenon (an occurance), which would never have been possible, if a provision for reservation of 1/3 seats for women had not been made.

From Development to Empowerment – The Ninth Five Year Plan

It was during the period of the Ninth Five-year Plan (1997-2002) that two significant developments took place in the field of women's development. The first relateds to the shift that took place in the framework (outline) for chalking out women's development programmes. Hitherto, women were either being treated as targets for development programmes or as participants. But not much attention was paid for creating an environment that would enable women to exercise their rights or enjoying their freedom. The Ninth Plan put forth the concept of Empowerment, which would create an enabling environment where, women can experience freedom not just in letter, but also in action. To achieve this goal a National Policy for the Empowerment of women was accepted by the Government of India in 2001. The second significant development, which took place during the Ninth Plan period, was the adoption of a Women's Component Plan. This Plan directed both the Central and State governments to earmark (set apart) atleast 30 per cent of the funds/ benefits in all sectors for women's development.

Women's Empowerment Year, 2001

The Government of India declared 2001 as the year of Women's Empowerment. Three primary objective were set to be achieved during this year. These were:

- Creating and raising large scale awareness of women's issues with active participation and involvement of women and men.
- Initiating and accelerating action for improving access to and control of resources by women.
- Creating an enabling environment for enhancing self-confidence and autonomy of women.

A number of policies and programmes were initiated during this year to ensure equal participation of women and men in the social, economic and political life of the nation.

Two prominent schemes that were launched for women during 2001 were: *Swayamsiddha* and *Swadhar*.

Swayamsiddha is an integrated programme, which supports the empowerment of women through a network of Self-Help Groups of women. It was hoped to bring together all the women related schemes of the central and state governments at the block level. The government also launched the *Swashakti* Project to help the setting up of women's Self-Helf Groups in villages by giving financial incentives. In many villages, Self-help Groups have ben doing great work in not only encouraging savings but also mobilizing women to fight against oppression in their families and village. Self-Help Groups also offer easy credit to members to start or improve small-scale business enterprises.

Swadhar was launched to provide rehabilitation to women in difficult circumstances such as destitute widows, women prisoners released from jail and without family support, women survivors of natural disaster and victims of sexual crimes. Shelter homes are planned to be constructed in which rehabilitation programmes will be offered on a holistic basis.

Activity: Visit a Self-Help Group, during one of its meetings and interact with the members. Prepare a report of about 250 words on their activities.

The Tenth Plan

The Tenth Plan (2002-07) became operational from April 1, 2002. A Working Group on Empowerment of women was constitute to prepare a base paper, to provide guidelines for future programmes for women's empowerment. This paper has made the following recommendations:

- Women must be helped to equip themselves to face the challenges being thrown up by globalization.

- Even though a number of development policies and programmes have been formulated to empower women, not all women could make use of these programmes because of the prevailing social discrimination against them. So investments on health, education and capacity building must be stepped up in future.
- During the last 10 years there has been a decline in expenditure on health, education and welfare. Since this affects women's development seriously, efforts must be made to increase investments on those sectors, which actually help women's development.

The Plans Reviewed

Since the planning period began in 1951, a number of programmes have been designed and implemented for women's empowerment. But all these efforts have not been able to remove gender discrimination inherent in such sectors as family life, health, education, employment and political participation. Dedicating one year to women's empowerment or one decade to girl children will not automatically bring about women's emancipation. There must be a commitment to make all these programmes functional in a way as to remove gaps between men and women on the one hand, and among women of different groups on the other. The need of the hour is an Action Plan, which believes in action and not just in talking about women.

Women's Empowerment Through Voluntary Actions

The women's movement in India has been a strong force in the struggle for empowerment of women. Prior to independence, organizations such as All India Women's Conference, Bharat Stri Mandal, Women's Indian Association, National Council of Women in India came into existence. These organizations no doubt raised issues of women's inequality, but their thought and action were not radical enough to question patriarchy. However, they organized campaigns against child marriage, *purdah* and demanded voting rights for women. These organizations were founded and managed mostly by women of middle or upper classes. By 1940 when the freedom struggle was at its height, the All India Women's Congress had raised this question. 'Today our men are clamouring for political rights at the hands of an alien government. Have they conceded to their wives, their own sisters, their daughters, 'flesh of their flesh, blood of their blood', social equality and economic justice'. The sentiment echoed in this question is that political freedom does not necessarity bring to women freedom from oppression. Though the pre-independence women's movement could not organize the masses, it had definitely set the stage for a strong women's movement to emerge in India after the country gained independence.

Even after independence, it took nearly 25 years for the emergence of women's groups and organizations, which took up women's issues from a feminist viewpoint. The observance of the International Women's decade between 1975-1985 led to the starting of courses on women's studies in many universities and colleges as well as action programmes organized by women's groups to sensitize the society to women's issues. A number of women's groups emerged in different parts of the country to raise basic questions about gender inequality and initiated action to counter these inequalities. These groups, known as autonomous (independent) women's groups did not have a connection with any political party. These autonomous women's groups did not believe in simply submitting representations or sending delegations to meet political leaders and request for action. On the contrary, they created a forum for women to meet and discuss issues that were affecting them and chalk out strategies to tackle all forms of oppression in society. Though educated middle class women took the initiative in forming and managing these groups, they took up the problems of working class women, tribal women, peasant women and dalit women. Yet another unique feature of the autonomous women's movement was the participation of women from all castes and classes. The autonomous women's groups also joined hands with other progressive movements, such as student movements, tribal movements, environment movements, anti-price rise movements or movements for equal wages.

Empowerment through action

The autonomous women's groups believe in fighting oppression, injustice and discrimination against women in all social institutions. The groups do not compromise their principles for any political, social or economic policies or programmes, which bring indignity to women. They are not entirely dependent upon government funds. They are fully aware of the fact that empowerment cannot be achieved until basic gender inequalities in family, economy, education and political institution are removed. The autonomous women's groups have two strategies for women's empowerment – awareness and action. Autonomous women's groups have taken up issues such as dowry, rape, family violence, alcoholism, sexual harassment at work place and many others. These groups are very active in their areas of location and work, and are being approached by women in need of support and help. They interact with the police, government representatives, employers or politicians to seek justice for women and uphold their self-respect.

The strength of the autonomous women's groups has been realized by the state and its agencies, which aften invite these groups to offer their advice on how matters relating to women could best be solved. The involvement of women's groups is also beling sought in creating awareness among different groups, which the state is trying to empower through its policies. Women's groups may join hands, but only after they are convinced that their basic principles are not compromised.

Women's Empowerment is a Process and not a Finished Product

In a country, which has a history of 3000 years of women's oppression, the attempts at emancipating women from this oppression are only about 175 years old. Given the volume and diversity of the problems, which women face in India it requires a very committed and continued effort on the part of all of us to reach the goal of women's empowerment. Empowerment is a light, which has to be lit in every heart and only them will it become a mass movement. Neither the state nor the women's groups, by themselves can solve all the problems, which women face. For women to be empowered we need an enlightened society, and that includes each one of us, wherever we are.

2

Gender Equality and Women's Empowerment

According to a CIDA report "Gender equality means that women and men have equal conditions for realizing their full human rights and potential to contribute to national political, economic, social and cultural development and benefit equally from the results...

Attaining gender equality demands a recognition that current social, economic, cultural, and political systems are gendered that women's unequal status is systemic and that it is necessary to incorporate women's specificity, priorities and values into all major social institutions." (CIDA)

Because of current disparities, however, equal treatment of women and men is insufficient as a strategy for gender equality. Equal treatment in the context of inequalities can mean the perpetuation of disparities. Achieving gender equality will require changes in institutional practices and social relations through which disparities are reinforced and sustained. It also requires specific action, which will lead to positive discrimination in favour of the depressed gender. ... Since women are the depressed gender it will require a strong voice for women in shaping their societies".

Gender equity is the process of being fair to women and men. To ensure fairness measures must often be available to compensate for historical and social disadvantages that prevent women and men from otherwise operating on a level playing field, measures that will empower women and achieve political, social, economic, cultural and environmental security (OECD, 1998).

Equality between women and men should be promoted in ways that are appropriate to each particular context. This begins with an understanding of the current status of women and men, their relations to each other and the interconnections between gender and other factors. In order to understand the quantitative disparities in the current status of men and women it is important to undertake gender analysis through sex segregated data of important social and economic sectors as well as women's position in decision making. Gender analysis can provide an understanding of the social relations and how inequality can be addressed.

Both men and women have a stake in building a more just society where all people are equally valued for their contributions. Yet, gender equality has often been seen as a 'women's issue' separate from men and 'gender' often been confused to mean women only. This is part of a tendency to consider men's characteristics as the norm and women's characteristics as different from the norm. Yet, both women and men are influenced by their gender and thus, ideas about the status of women are interrelated with ideas about the status of men. In short, change for women means change for men and vice versa. However, since men are considered superior to women, gender equality is approached from the point of empowering women to become equal to men.

Gender equality is not only a social / gender justice issue and a measure of equal participation, it is an important component for economic development. Because inequality of access to development resources and to decision-making power between women and men results in lower contribution to development by women, who are half of the labor force, than that of men. No society can exploit its full potential for development if half of its labor force is less developed than the other half. The United Nations identified this as a major reason for slow economic development of developing countries as early as at the end of its First Development Decade (1960s) and emphasized on the number countries to identify the status of women in their respective countries to identify gender economic and social inequalities and evolve strategies to reduce the inequalities. All member states of the UN are committed to gender equality. Research in this area revealed, however, that gender inequalities exist in all societies-developed and underdeveloped in different forms and degrees. this is when women of the world got united to raise a voice against inequality, which is reflected not only in lower economic and social positions of women but is also the major cause of gender violence.

The Human development Report of the UN published every year to measure human development, which according to it is a major contributor to development. The Report also stresses on the need for gender equality and empowerment of women in order to achieve equality. It has developed indices for measuring improvement in these indicators. Equality is considered by the UN as a fundamental input in human development and subsequent economic development.

Gender equality as a development goal

Gender equality is both as essential element of any development process and a result of sustainable development. Development efforts should not only aim to advance equality between women and men as an outcome, but should also advance equality throughout by applying gender analysis in planning, consultations, design, implementation and assessment.

Women's empowerment

Since it is women who predominantly experience inequality (inferiority), empowerment supports women to become more aware of the unfair power relations they face. Empowerment allows both men and women to take control over their lives by gaining skills, setting their own agendas and building self-confidence and self-reliance. It also means that women have increased control over their lives by acquiring a voice to challenge and overcome the inequality they experience. Empowerment is both a process and a result that cannot be achieved by an individual or organization for someone else. A woman can only empower herself, although organizations and agencies around the world can play a role in supporting this journey and providing an enabling environment. Gender equality is both an essential element of any development process and a result of sustainable development. Development efforts should not only aim to advance equality between women and men as an outcome, but should also advance equality throughout by applying gender analysis in planning, consultations, design, implementation and assessment.

It is one of the goals of Millennium Development (4), which proposed to : Eliminate gender disparity in primary and secondary education, preferably by 2005, and to all levels of education no later than 2015. The Indicators for achievement of Millennium Development Goal 4 are equality in:

- Ratio of girls to boys in primary, secondary, and tertiary education
- Ratio of literate women to men ages 15 to 24
- Share of women in wage employment in the nonagricultural sector
- Proportion of seats held by women in national parliament

The Government of India is committed to achieve the goal of gender equality, which is also enshrined in the

Constitutional rights. Furthermore it has committed itself to ensure gender equality in several international conventions and Beijing Platform for Action. Almost all the political parties have inserted gender equality, in some form or the other, as an objective in their party election manifestoes. To day no person or politician can oppose gender equality as an undesirable development goal.

Without going into international comparisons, I shall restrict myself to data over-time on India to measure the extent of inequality, measures taken to reduce it through policy measures and empowerment of women as well as the effects of the measures taken so far and the road ahead. We can find answers to most of these questions through gender analysis of data on economic, social and political position of women. Sex segregated data are not available for all sectors before 1971. However, importance of collection of such data was impressed by the report of the Committee on the Status of Women 1975 and since then special efforts have been made to collect sex-segregated data. The Report, "Towards Equality" (1975) was the first exhaustive document, which brought out extreme gender inequalities in the country and the need to change this status. The Report was presented to the Parliament, which recommended that the P.M. take specific administrative and legislative measures at removing economic and social injustices and disabilities and discrimination to which women continued to be subjected even after a quarter century of Independence. It is interesting to note that the Parliament's recommendations did not take note of gender inequalities as such but was concerned about injustices and discrimination and disabilities which when removed would no doubt create a more enabling environment but will not necessarily lead to equality because importance of measures for gender equity were overlooked by the Parliament in its recommendations. It is only in subsequent research and pressure from the women's movement that these measures have been introduced in piecemeal.

Since then through gender specific government policy measures, international gender focused development aid and collective actions by women's groups have led to reduction of inequalities somewhat. The results of this collective efforts of almost quarter of a century (1975-2001) has been captured through collection and analysis of exhaustive data in the report prepared by Dr. Sarla Gopalan (retired Secretary Department of Women and Child Development Govt of India) "Towards Equality – The Unfinished Agenda – Status of Women in Indis - 2001" commissioned by the National Commission for Women. Gender analysis of the data on several sectors of Indian society reveals, however, that after 55 years of Independence gender equality is nowhere in view.

What has changed since Todards Equality?

Following policy measures are significant:

- A section included on Women's development in the 6th Five Year Plan and each Plan subsequent to it. The focus in the Plan priorities in this section has progressively changed from women's welfare programmes to women's empowerment and gender equality issues including insisting on all sectoral ministries to appoint a gender specilist and evaluate their budgetary allocations for gender budgeting.
- Setting up of National Human Rights Commission (NHRC) & National Commission for Women (NWC). While the NHRC takes up all human right violations, a slogan has been coined by women activists that human rights are women's rights. Thus NHRC thus is more often faced with cases of gender violence. NCW has been constituted especially on demand from women activists in order to have national level and states level commissions, which will recommend policies, which will bring about gender equality and women's empowerment. These are spoke persons on women's issues. However, because of its limited power and being under the government the NCW has often been seen to

be not doing enough to strengthen women's voices. At states level few Commissions are strong enough to mobilize public opinion and manage state level political bosses for effective pro-women policies and programmes.

- Amendments to existing laws and new lows passed by the parliament with gender perspective.

The laws passed before and since CSWI report which focused on protection of women rights and safety were:

(1) In the area of personal rights, besides the Hindu Women's Right to property – 1922 & 1937, and Hindu Succession Act 1956, Shariat law/Muslim marriage Act 1939 and the Hindu code Bill 1952, the additional laws passed to protect women's personal rights since 1971 are the Hindu women's succession Act 1978–Hindu Succession Act (Andhra Pradesh) 1985. Hindu Succession Act 2005. The 1956 Act did not give equal rights to married women in self acquired property and even the unequal share was not given to them by use of the instrument of 'will' and/or by coercing and daughters to give up their share in favor of their brothers. Also daughters had no right in the inherited property. Andhra Pradesh was the first to plug these loopholes in the Succession Act in 1986. Recently the Hindu Women's Succession Act amendment 2005 has given full equality to women in inherited property, which includes agricultural land.

(2) In 1978 the Child Marriage Restraint Act of 1929 amended to raise the age of marriage for girls from 14 to 18 and that of the boys from 15 to 21.

(3) The Dowry Prohibition Act (DPA) enacted in 1961 was amended in 1984 and again in 1986 to make it a non-bailable (cognizable) offense under section 304 B and 498 A which made strict punishment possible particularly in case of dowry deaths.

(4) While Hindu women are protected in case of divorce which itself was made more difficult under the Hindu Code Bill, Muslim women are not under the purview of

the act and when applied in case of Shahbano for maintenance there was protest from the Muslim community for interference in their personal laws and a special Muslim women (protection on divorce) Act was passed in 1986. Because of uneven treatment of women from minority communities there has been a strong demand for Uniform Civil Code.

(5) Adoption, Guardianship's custody, Hindu Minority and guardianship Act 1956 gives unequal, exclusive right to the father. The Act was challenged in 1999 in the Supreme Court, which by its decision set precedence for mothers and father to have equal right.

(6) Domestic Violence against women cases so far were registered under IPC 498 A under which few criminals have been punished and courts take ages to decide the cases. Under the new act 'Prevention of Domestic Violence Act 2005' in cases registered under the act women have very broad rights and it is mandatory for the courts to decide the cases within a stipulate period. The Act has been termed as the Magna Carta for women's liberation.

(7) Regulation & Prevention of Misuse of sex determination (RPMSD) Act 1994: Unfavorable sex ratio, particularly in 0-5 age group through female feticide has led the government to pass the RPMSD act. Under the act both the parents and the doctors assisting in feticide are liable for severe punishment including jail. However not a single conviction has been reported during the 11 years since the law was passed.

(8) Rape is a major and a very severe form of violence against women. Rape is a cognizable offence. Section 376 of IPC deals with all cases of rape including that of minors. Section 354 of IPC deals with As a result of Mathura (a minor) Rape case 114A amendment in Evidence Act was added, it was approved that the courts shall not ask for evidence in rape cases. There are very strict rape laws with immdiate imprisonment and punishment up to 7 years. There has been a discussion

on extending death penalty in case of rape. However, it has been opposed by women's groups who insist that implementation of the existing laws and speedy verdicts by the courts will be enough deterrent and death penalty will only further reduce conviction rate; currently conviction rate is very low and cases drag on for years.

(9) Bill on Sexual Harrassment at work place (with a very broad definition of 'work place') is expected to be passed in the winter session of the Parliament.

(10) Immoral Traffic prevention Act 1986 prevents trafficking in women & children and child prostitution.

There has been rapid progress in amending laws and making new laws for protection of women and for stricter punishment for crimes against women. However, as laws have become stringent there is increase in reported crimes against women. However, large majority of cases are not registered and from among the ones registered a number of them are withdrawn and the ones that reach up to the courts few get completed and criminals punished.

But once the cases go up to the judiciary, judges have been liberal in interpretation of the laws in dealing with cases involving women's issues.

Policies for Gender Equality and Empowerment of Women:

The National Policy on Education (1992) brought focus on girl's education – Education being mother of all Institutions. The data on Literacy Rates by sex show much greater increase in female literacy than the males (Table 1) rapid increase in number of girls Per 100 boys at Primary and Secondary Levels (Table 2) and at University and Higher levels of Education (Table 3). Education is the main empowerment instrument for women.

Educational Development

Literacy rate of female has gone up from 8.9% in 1951 to 54.2% in 2001. Both, rise in income and increase in the age

Table 1 Literacy Rates – India; 1951-2001

Year	*Persons*	*Male*	*Female*
1951	18.33	27.16	8.86
1961	28.31	40.40	15.34
1971	34.45	45.95	21.97
1981	43.67	56.50	29.85
1991*	52.21	64.13	39.29
1997@	62.00	73.13	50.29
2001#	65.38	75.85	54.16

Source: Registrar General, India, Note: Literacy Rate for 1951, 1961, 1971 and 1981 related to population aged five years and above. Census could not be held in Assam in 1981 and J& K in 1991.

@ An analysis based on NSSO Survey 1998, National Literacy Mission.

Census, 2001

Table 2: Number of Girls per 100 Boys in Primary and Secondary Schools 1950-1997

Year	*Primary Classes*	*Secondary Classes*
1950-51	39	16
1960-61	48	23
1970-71	60	35
1980-81	63	44
1991-1992	71	50
2001-2002	90	na

at marriage are responsible for it as well as government's implementation of compulsory universal primary education and non-formal education programs like National Elementary Education Mission, Operation Black Board, and Sarva Shiksha Abhiyan and innumerable NGOs initiatives. The latest policy announcement of investment of Rs. 80,000 corors on universal Secondary Education in the next five years is a major initiative of the Government of India. Contribution of NGOs in imparting literacy to adult women and drop out girls is of significant.

Disparities between male and female education still exist. However, the importance of education has been brought out by The National Committee on Women's Education 1959 and National Plan of Action 1976. National

Table 3: Index of Growth in Enrolment of Girls in Higher Education 1970-71 & 1993.

	94	
Category		1993-94
Graduation	Total	292
	Female	445
Post Graduation	T	331
	F	456
Research	T	470
	F	784
Diploma/ Certificate	T	231
	F	300
1. Total for general education	T	296
	F	447
Professional education		
Graduation	T	302
	F	465
Post Graduation	T	425
	F	632
Research	T	467
	F	164
Diploma/ Certificate	T	219
	F	222
2. Total For Professional	T	316
	F	458
Grand Total for 1+2	T	298
	F	448

Female as %age of total 1970-71 22% 33%

Source: Based on Data of the University Grants Commission quoted in NCRT Report 'Fifty Years of Women's Education in India' (1947-97)

policy on Education 1986. Program of Action on Education for Women's Equality brought out the importance of education for empowerment of women, development and gender equality. National Development Council Committee on Literacy – 1992-93 reported on a Word Bank study in 29 countries, which showed an inverse relationship between child mortality and women's education and direct correlation between immunization status of children and female education.

Education thus is not simply a matter of social justice but more a matter of economic growth, social well-being and social stability. The Committed also found that absence of facilities for higher levels of education leads to higher drop out rate at primary levels of education.

The drop out rates at primary school levels is high for both boys and girls and was almost equal in 1996-97. In fact in secondary class the drop out rates of boys is higher than that of girls. (Gopalan: Table 5.10 page 148).

One of major recommendation of the BPFA is allocation of sufficient resources on education. The GOI committed itself to double the expenditure on education from 3% to 6% of GDP. However, ten years later (in spite of levy of an education cess of 2%) the expenditure on education as %age of the GDP has gone up to 4%.

The growth in the number of institutions between 1950-51 & 1998-99 for different levels of education is given below

Inspite of inscrease in educational institutions, India will achieve universal primary education target 30 years after

Table: 4 Growth in Recognized education institutions

	Primary	*UP*	*HS*	*College*	*Professional*	*University*
1950-51 = 100	209671	13596	7416	370	208	27
1998-99 Index	626737 334	190166 715	112438 660	7494 4937	2113 9843	237 1139

Korea and 20-years after Malaysia (UNDP Human Development Report 1999).

National Policy on Empowerment of Women.

The 73rd & 74th Amendment to the Constitution reserving 1/3 of seats for women in elected village & urban local bodies passed in 1972 and 1974 have brought millions of women across the country into local level decision making bodies not only as members of the institutions but also as their heads and chairpersons (Table 5 and 5-A).

Besides while the proportion of women voters voting has been lower than that of the men, the difference in the proportion has narrowed from 15 percentage points to just 8 (Table 6).

Women's representation in higher level decision making bodies i.e. in the lower and upper house of the Parliament (Table 7) and in State legislatures (Table 8) show that women constitute a miniscule proportion of the total members. However, their proportion in Parliament (Lok Sabha and Rajya Sabha) has gone up from 6.1% in 1989 to 8.4% by 1999. In 2004 it is 9.1%. However, in state legislatures has either gone down or has remained stagnant. Efforts at passage of the Constitutional Amendment for 33% reservation of seats for women in national and state level legislatures has been strongly opposed by all political parties in spite of commitment in their party election manifestoes gender equality and one-third representation of women in all decision making bodies.

Their representation in Council of Ministers has remained steady at 10% for decades. (Table 9). However there number among cabinet ministers is never more than one member. Even among party executives the proportion of women ranges from 5-12%; lowest being among leftist parties who have never have had a woman as member of the Politburo until very recently. However, there are a number of political parties headed by women - Congress I, Samta, BSP, (AIADMK) and AITC (Gopalan Table 9/7 p. 290).

Table 5: Women Representatives in Panchayati Raj Institutions (Percentage), 2002

S. No.	India/ States/Union Territories	1997			2002		
		GP	TP	ZP	GP	TP	ZP
	1	2	3	4	5	6	7
1.	Andhra Pradesh	33.84	37.01	33.21	33.00	33.65	33.24
2.	Arunachal Pradesh	Arunachal Pradesh Panchayati Raj Act not yet passed					
3.	Assam**	18.01	26.09	-	33.45	34.73	30.00
4.	Bihar	Post 73rd Amendment Election not held in the State, not available					
5.	Chhattisgarh	-	-	-	33.74	34.33	34.67
6.	Delhi	NCT government propose conduct of Panchayat Elections					
7.	Goa	36.53	-	-	31.76	-	34.00
8.	Gujarat	17.29	33.43	33.38	33.35	33.48	33.54
9.	Haryana	30.74	35.31	80.53	33.59	34.65	34.71
10.	Himachal Pradesh	32.93	33.59	33.33	36.78	33.90	34.66
11.	Jammu & Kashmir	State proposes adopting 73rd Amendment					
12.	Jharkand	Current Figure not available					
13.	Karnataka	43.79	40.21	36.45	44.86	42.24	38.09

14.	Kerala	Current Figure not availbale			36.21	38.40	34.20
15.	Madhya Pradesh	32.93	34.84	2.99	33.82	33.44	33.79
16.	Maharashtra	33.33	33.31	33.31	33.33	36.06	33.73
17.	Manipur	35.67	-	36.07	35.48	-	36.07
18.	Meghalaya	TraditionalCouncils performs duties of local government.					
19.	Mizoram						
20.	Nagaland						
21.	Orissa	33.35	33.35	33.26	35.88	35.14	34.66
22.	Punjab	35.69	Election due	35.69	32.78	31.90	
23.	Rajasthan	29.73	31.67	3.21	34.52	36.29	36.11
24.	Sikkim	37.34	-	30.43	36.88	-	31.52
25.	Tamil Nadu	25.07	35.31	3.40	26.86	26.94	26.37
26.	Tripura	33.55	34.18	34.29	33.33	35.81	34.15
27.	Uttaranchal	-	-	-	-	-	-
28.	Uttar Pradesh	15.08	23.11	23.60	-	-	-
29.	West Bengal	36.33	35.18	33.94	22.46	22.42	21.58

Union Territories							
30.	Andaman & Nicobar Islands	34.33	-	33.33	34.39	37.31	33.33
31.	Chandigarh	Current Figures are not available			33.95	40.00	30.00
32.	Dadra & Nagar Haveli	34.07	-	25.00	36.29	-	33.33
33.	Daman & Diu	39.68	-	33.33	26.98	-	40.00
34.	Lakshadweep	37.97	-	36.36	37.97	-	36.36
35.	Pondicherry	Not available. Post 73rd Amendment Elections not held at the State					
	India	6.40	8.86	3.38	3.66	2.70	2.99

Note: Annual Report 2000-01, Ministry of Rural Development, Government of India.

Source: India, Ministry of Human Resource Development, Department of Women and Child Development. (2004). Government of India, II & IIIrd Periodic Report on the Convention on the Elimination of All Forms of Discrimination against Women: CEDAW Periodic Report. New Delhi. P.86.

Table 5 - A Women in Panchayati Raj Institutions (1995-2001)

(Figures in thousand)

Year	*Women*	*Men*	*Total*
1995*	318 (33.5%)	630	948
2001*	725 (26.6)	1,997	2,722

Table 6: Percentage of Female and Male voters casting their vote in each election in India

Election Year	*Percentage of Female Voters*	*Percentage of Male Voters*
1952	-	-
1962	29.07%	59.68%
1967	41.79%	65.12%
1972	44.37%	66.03%
1977	43.26%	62.15%
1980	39.28%	58.48%
1985	41.37%	58.04%
1993	49.72%	68.22%
1998	53.35%	66.45%

Women in higher civil services: The proportion of women in government services has gone up from 11% to 15%. In senior level services, women constitute less than 10% both in IAS (around 9%) and Indian Customs and Central Excise service (around 7%) and in Indian Police service (2%). Their proportion in Indian Statistical services and in the Central Secretariat services is also 5-7%). In some of the other services their proportion ranges between 15-20%. Their higher proportion in the Indian Foreign Service is noticeable. Their proportion in some of the other services like the Police is almost negligible, (Table 10) While women among State High Courts judges is low but has been increasing but among Supreme Court judges there has never been more than one woman. (Tables 11.

Economic Empowerment of Women

Women experience barriers in access to economic resources land, natural resources - wood, water-capital, credit technology etc. Also most of the economic activities they do are not counted as work because they are not paid for it. Besides they have to spend lot of their time in household chores to which no economic values has been put so far.

Table - 7: Women's Representation in Parliament 1952-1998

Table - 7: Women's Representation in Parliamane 1952-1998

Year	Lok Sabha			Rajya Sabha*		
	Seats	Women MPs	% Women MPs	Seats	Women MPs	% Women MPs
1952	499	22	4.41	219	16	07.31
1957	500	27	5.40	237	18	07.59
1962	503	34	6.76	238	18	07.56
1967	523	31	5.93	240	20	08.33
1971	544	19	3.49	244	25	10.25
1980	544	28	5.15	244	24	09.84
1984	544	44	8.09	244	28	11.48
1989	517	27	5.22	245	24	09.80
1991	544	39	7.17	245	38	15.51
1996	543	39	7.18	223	19	08.52
1998	543	43	7.92	245	15	06.12
Average	527	31	5.91	239	22	09.11

According to time use surveys the time spent by women and men (completed in six states during the year June 1998-June 1999)) 55% of the work time was contributed by women and only 45% by men. However, women are at the margin of economic activities in unorganized, low skill, low paid jobs, thus large majority of women are not counted as workers. Globalization increases vulnerability of those at the margins of economies. Many women have been forced to accept low pay and poor working conditions and thus have become the preferred workers.

The process of globalization involves economic reforms in terms of stabilization measures and structural adjustment. Stabilization includes reduction in budget deficits - involving expenditure control, devaluations, imports control etc. Structural adjustments involve deregulation and liberalization - liberalization of foreign trade delicensing of industries - control on inflow of foreign capital, slashing subsidies etc.

Protected economies with extensive periods of control feel more the pain and slow process of adjustments. Economic measures for liberalization of the economy in India have included sale of uneconomic public enterprises, reduction in size of the government. After a period of devaluation, the rupee now has remained stabilized. In short term, liberalization leads to increase in unemployment, however.

Work Participation Rates:

Exact change in work participation rate for women is rather difficult to guage because of frequent changes in the definition of "worker" used in the Population Censuses - which give the most reliable and exhaustive country wide data. The changes in definition effects the count of workers in agriculture and unorganized industrial sectors where large majority of the women work. Thus change in definition effects

Table 9: Representation of Women in the Central Council of Ministers, 1985–2005

Year	*Females*	*Males*	*Total*
1985	4 (10.0%)	36	40
2001	8 (10.8%)	66	74
2005	7 (10.4%)		

Note: Figures within parentheses indicate percentage to total.

* Data refers to 9 States - Gujarat, Haryana, Karnataka, Kerala, Madhya Pradesh, Punjab, Rajasthan, Tripura and West Bengal.

* For whole of India (as on 18.10.2001)

Source: National Informations Center, Parliament House, New Delhi.

Table 8: Declining Representation of Women in State Legislatures 1952-1997 (% of women MLAs)

State	1952	1957	1960-1965	1967-1969	1970-1975	1977-1978	1979-1983	1984-1988	1989-1992	1993-1997	1998-1999	State. Avg.
Andhra Pradesh	2.9	3.7	3.3	3.8	9.1	3.4	4.1	3.4	3.7	2.7	9.5	4.6
Arunachal Pradesh	****	****	****	****	****	0.0	3.3	6.7	3.3	3.3	1.7	3.0
Assam	0.5	4.6	3.8	4.0	7.0	0.8	0.8	4.0	4.0	4.8	****	3.2
Bihar	3.6	9.4	7.9	2.2	3.8	4.0	3.7	4.6	2.8	3.4	****	4.3
Goa	****	****	****	6.7	3.3	3.3	0.0	0.0	5.0	10.0	5.0	4.4
Gujarat	****	****	8.4	4.8	3.2	****	2.7	8.8	2.2	1.1	2.2	4.0
Haryana	****	****	****	7.4*	6.2	4.4	7.8	5.6	6.7	4.4	****	6.2
Himachal Pradesh	0.0	****	****	0.0	5.9	1.5	4.4	4.4	5.9	4.4	8.8	4.2
Jammu & Kashmir	****	****	0.0	0.0	5.3	1.3	0.0	1.3	****	2.3	****	1.5
Karnataka	2.0	8.7	8.7	3.2	5.1	4.0	0.9	3.6	4.5	3.1	2.3	4.3
Kerala	0.0	4.8	3.9	0.8	1.5	0.7	3.2	5.7	5.7	9.3	****	3.6
Madhya Pradesh	2.1	10.8	4.9	3.4	5.4	3.1	5.6	9.7	3.4	3.8	8.1	5.4
Maharashtra	1.9	6.3	4.9	3.3	9.3	2.8	6.6	5.6	2.1	3.8	4.2	4.6
Manipur	****	****	****	****	0.0*	****	0.0	0.0	1.7	0.0	****	0.3
Meghalaya	****	****	****	****	1.7	1.7	0.0	3.3	****	1.7	5.0	2.2

Mizoram	****	****	****	****	0.0	3.3	3.3	2.5	0.0	0.0	0.0	1.2
Nagaland	****	****	****	0.0	****	****	0.0	1.7	****	0.0	****	0.5
Orissa	9.6	3.6	1.4	3.6	1.4*	4.8	3.4	6.1	4.8	5.4	****	4.0
Punjab	2.2	5.8	5.2	1.0*	5.8	2.6	5.1	3.4	6.1	4.8	5.4	****
Rajasthan	0.0	5.1	4.5	3.3	7.1	4.0	5.0	8.0	5.5	4.5	7.0	5.0
Sikkim	****	****	****	****	****	****	0.0	0.0	6.3	3.1	3.1	2.5
Tamil Nadu	03	5.9	3.9	1.7	2.1	0.9	2.1	3.4	9.0	3.8	****	3.6
Tripura	****	****	****	0.0	3.3	1.7	6.7	3.3	****	1.7	****	3.0
Uttar Pradesh	1.2	5.8	4.4	2.8*	5.9	2.6	5.6	7.3	3.3*	4.0*	****	4.1
West Bengal	0.8	3.6	4.8	2.9*	1.6*	1.4	2.4	4.4	7.1	6.8	****	3.4
Delhi	4.2	****	****	****	7.1	7.1	7.1	****	****	4.3	12.9	7.3
Pondicherry	****	****	6.7	3.3	0.0	0.0	3.3	3.3	1.7	3.3	****	2.6
Period Average	1.8	6.3	4.9	2.9	4.4	2.8	3.8	5.3	4.5	4.0	6.0	4.1

Female Work Participation Rate (FWPR) than Male Work Participation Rate (MWPR).

However, the date show that fwpr has almost doubled between 1971-2001 from 13.9 to 25.7% (Table 12); the wpr of the males, however, has remained almost unchanged around 52%. The main reason for increase in fwpr has been more scientific methods of countine 'workers'. There has, however, been increase in wpr of both rural and urban women. The rapid increase in education and skill development of women and their capacity to work at lower wages has also contributed the increase in the fwpr.

Distribution by sector

Proportion of women workers in agriculture has remained almost unchanged although there has been a one-percentage point decline in agricultural labor and a one-percentage point increase as cultivators. There has been a one percentage point decline in women working in the household sector which has not been fully compensated by increase in 'Other than Household Industry" which recoded an increase of only one-quarter of one percentage point. The major addition has been in women working in the 'Other services' sector where 8.26 percent of women work as against around 7% in 1981 (Table 13).

Although the percentage of women among total workers in the organized sector has gone up steadily from 11% in 1971 to 17.4% in 1999. Table 14 shows, however, that they are concentrated in the public sector and in services and in industries where wage levels are low. The employment in the public sector has reached a saturation point, however. Women's employment has not increased in most of the sectors except in trade, hotels and restaurants and in casual labor and there has been feminization of poverty.

Poverty Eradication Programmes include almost 13 schemes of which DWACRA is specially targeted to women.

Table 10: Number of Judges by Sex in Supreme Court/ High Courts as on 2003

Name of the Court	Number of Judges		
	Female	Male	Total
Supreme Court	1	24	25
High Courts			
Allahabad	1	69	70
Andhra Pradesh	2	32	34
Bombay	3	49	52
Calcutta	1	41	42
Chhattisgarh	-	4	4
Delhi	1	27	42
Guwahati	-	12	12
Gujarat	1	30	31
Himachal Pradesh	1	5	6
Jammu & Kashmir	-	11	11
Jharkhand	-	12	12
Karnataka	1	31	32
Kerala	1	25	26
Madhya Pradesh	1	23	24
Madras	1	30	31
Orissa	-	12	12
Patna	1	23	24
Punjab & Haryana	1	30	31
Rajasthan	1	25	26
Sikkim	-	2	2
Uttaranchal	-	4	4
Total	17	497	514

Note: Department of Justice, Ministry of Law and Justice and Company Affairs.

***Source*:** India, Ministry of Statistics and Programme Implementation, Central Statistical Organization. (2003). Women and Men in India 2002. New Delhi. P.98.

Note: Figures within parentheses indicate percentage of total.

* Data refers to 9 States - Gujarat, Haryana, Karnataka, Kerala, Madhya Pradesh, Punjab, Rajasthan, Tripura and West Bengal.

* For whole of India (as on 18.10.2001).

***Source*:** Ministry of Rural Development, Government of India, New Delhi.

In 1999-2000 several of the schemes were merged into one scheme SGSY and several others were restructured. Laws were passed for protection of 'Home Based Workers' in some industries e.g. Beedi workers. In 1996 the Government of India signed the ILO Convention for protection of HBW and also prepared a National Policy on Home Based Workers. Several labor laws have been passed during the past 40-year, which give equal wages, maternity relief and unemployment insurance etc.

Table 11: Percentage of Women in Civil Services personnel

Category	*Year*	*Women % of Total*
Indian administrative Service	1993	9.3
	1996	9.9
Indian Audits & Accounts Service	1993	15.7
	1995	17.8
Indian Customs and Excise	1993	6.7
	1996	7.8
Indian Economics Service	1993	18.8
	1996	16.2
Indian Foreign Service	1993	10.1
	1995	13.7
Indian Information Service	1994	15.8
	1996	15.6
Indian Postal Service	1993	17.5
	1996	21.4

The government has launched innumerable schemes for increase in employment and income of the poor rural population with some specifically aimed at women e.g. DWACRA. The latest Rural Employment Guarantee bill passed by the Parliament recently reserves 33% of additional employment for women.

Table 12: Work Participation Rates, 1971-1991, India

Workers	*India*			*Rural*			*Urban*		
	Total	*Female*	*Male*	*Total*	*Female*	*Male*	*Total*	*Female*	*Male*
1971 (Main & secondary)	34.0	13.9	52.7	36.1	15.9	53.8	29.6	7.2	48.9
1981 (Main & marginal)	36.8	19.8	52.6	38.9	23.2	53.8	30.0	8.3	49.1
1991 (Main & marginal)	37.5	22.3	51.6	40.0	27.1	52.5	30.2	9.7	48.9
2001	39.3	25.7	51.9	42.6	31.0	52.4	32.2	11.5	50.8

Source: Census of India, 1971, 1981, 1991 and 2001

Table 13: Occupational Shift of Workers Through Decadal Census, 1971-1991

Category	*Persons*			*Male*			*Female*		
	1971	*1981*	*1991*	*1971*	*1981*	*1991*	*1981*	*1981*	*1991*
I. Cultivators	43	41.46	38.41	46	43.71	39.63	30	33.09	34.22
II. Agricultural Laborers	26	25.12	26.44	21	19.57	21.06	50	46.34	44.93
III. Livestock, Forestry, Fishing, Hunting, Plantations, orchards and Allied activities	2	2.25	1.90	2	2.37	1.99	3	1.83	1.60
IV. Mining and Quarrying	1	0.58	0.62	1	0.63	0.70	-	0.35	0.34
V. Manufacturing, Processing, Servicing and Repairs:	4	3.45	2.42	4	3.18	2.09	4	4.57	3.53
	6	7.85	7.76	7	8.91	8.89	3	3.60	3.88
a) Household industry									
b) Other than household industry									
VI. Construction	1	1.66	1.95	1	1.87	2.32	1	0.87	0.66

VII. Trade and Commerce	6	6.33	7.46	6	7.41	8.98	2	2.04	2.26
VIII. Transport, Storage* and Communications	2	2.75	2.81	3	3.36	3.54	-	0.37	0.32
IX. Other Services	9	8.55	10.23	9	8.99	10.80	7	6.94	8.26
	100	100.0	100.0	100	100.0	100.0	100	100.0	100.0

Source: Census of India, 1971 (Series 1-India Part II-B (i) General Economic Table). Women in India, A Statistical Profile - 1997, Department of Women and Child Development.

Other policies announced but no plan of action or implementation of the policy has been the fate of the followings:

- National Plan of Action for women 1976.
- National perspective plan 1988 - 2000.
- National Plan of Action for the Girl Child 1991-2000.

Other Good Initiatives

Setting up of Department of Women and Child development in the Ministry for Human Resource development has led to gender sensitization in budgetary allocations and in design of government supported development programmes. The department functions like a watchdog in the government.

Central Social Welfare Board and Rashtriya Mahilakosh (which was set up as a result of the findings of the Shram Shakti Report) have welfare and micro credit as their main functions towards empowerment of women.

Parliamentary committee on Empowerment of women was set up in 2000, the year of Women's Empowerment in India. The Committee examines measures taken by the Union Government for women's Empowerment and in Five Years Plans and on gender budgeting.

Women and Health

Table on expectation of life at birth of men and women shows that while the female expected to live longer than the males during 1901-21, their life expectancy fell below that of the males from 1931 to 1961, it was about the same in 1971. However, since 1971, the female expectation of life has increased more than that of men and in 2001 women expected to live three years longer than the men (Table 15).

Data on Infant mortality rates by sex over the years (1972-1998) given in (Table 16) do not show any pattern. However, the data on sex ratio given in the Table below (Table 17) show a continuous decline from 1001 to 1961 when

Table 14: Proportion of Women among the Total Workers in the Organized Sector and Percentage Increase 1971-1999

Category	*1997*			*1999*			*Variation*
	Total	*Women*	*% of Women*	*Total*	*Women*	*% of Women*	*In women employees 1999/1971 (%)*
Public Sector							
Central Government	27.60	0.78	2.82	33.13	2.52	7.60	323%
Stage Government	40.50	3.53	8.50	74.58	13.79	18.50	390%
Quasi-Central and State	19.23	0.86	4.50	63.86	5.89	9.22	684%
Local bodies	18.78	3.44	18.30	22.59	5.91	26.16	171%
Total	107.10	8.61	8.03	194.15	28.11	14.50	327%
Private Sector							
Large establishments	67.40	10.63	15.77	77.70	17.92	23.06	195%
Small establishments	9.28	2.77	29.85				
Total	67.40	10.63	15.77	86.98	20.69	23.12	195%
Gramd Total	174.50	19.24	11.02	281.13	48.30	17.18	251%

Source: Directorate General of Employment and Training.

Table 15: Life Expectancy at Birth of Males and females during the past 100 years 1991-2001

Year	*M*	*F*	*Both*	*F-M*
1901-11	22.6	23.3	22.9	0.7
1911-21	19.4	20.9	20.1	1.5
1921-31	26.9	26.6	26.8	-.3
1931-41	32.1	31.4	31.8	-.7
1941-51	32.4	31.7	32.1	-.7
1951-61	41.9	40.6	41.3	-1.3
1961-71	46.4	44.7	45.6	-1.7
1970-75	50.5	49.0	49.7	-1.5
1976-80	52.5	52.1	52.3	-.4
1981-85	55.4	55.7	55.4	.3
1986-90	57.7	58.1	57.7	.4
1987-91	58.1	58.6	58.3	.5
1991-95	59.7	60.9	60.3	1.2
1992-96	60.1	61.4	60.7	1.3
*1996-01	62.4	63.4	62.9	1.0
**2001	63.9	66.9	65.3	3.0

Source: Country Statement, International Conference on Population Development, Cairo, 1994 and Registrar General of India.

* Planning Commission July 2000

** Statistical Outline of India 2003-04, Tata Services Ltd, p.31.

it was 841. The ratio has improved some since then but is still low at, having gone up from 927 to 933 in 1991.

They are however higher in rural areas then in urban and higher in the sourthern states than in the northern states. The high expectation of life at birth of females and continuous low sex-ration only indicate the oft-focused issue of female feticide. The earlier explanation of female children if allowed to be born, more or less live as long as the males. However such low ration of girl children to boy children born only reconfirms wide prevalence of female feticide. The sex ratio of children born has no relevance to poverty; it has been noticed in poor states as well as the richest. (Mapping

Table 16: Estimated infant mortality rates by sex and residence, India 1972-1998

Year	*Total*			*Rural*			*Urban*		
	Total	*Males*	*Females*	*Total*	*Males*	*Females*	*Total*	*Males*	*Females*
1972	140	132	148	151	141	161	85	85	85
1978	125	120	131	136	130	142	70	69	71
1983	105	105	105	114	114	115	66	69	63
1988	94	96	94	102	103	102	62	65	59
1993	74	73	75	82	81	84	45	47	44
1994	74	75	73	80	80	78	52	53	51
1998	72	70	74	77	76	79	45	42	49

Source: Women in India - A Statistical Profile, 1997. Sample Registration System, Fertility & Mortality Indicators - 1982-1993, Registrar General of India; SRS Bulletins 1996, 1998, RGI.

Table 17: Sex ratio of Population (F/M 1000) 1901-2001

Year	1901	1911	1921	1931	1941	1951	1961	1971	1981	1991	2001
F/M	972	964	955	950	945	946	841	930	933	927	933

Source: Registrar General of India 1991 series 1 and 2001- Provisional Population Totals

Adverse Child Sex Ratio in India November 2003 UNPF, Ministry of Health and office of the Census Commissioner of India).

The decline in sex ratio has occurred in states having large concentration of the population, is concentrated more in the northern states than in the south and includes some of the riches district of Punjab, Haryana and Delhi. In a recent study supported by UNFPA on 'Infanticide in Rajasthan - 'Causes and Practices' conducted by VIHAAN, Society for child Development, the sex ratio has been declining from 1961 to 1991. In 2001 it recorded a small increase over 1991. However, in 2001, 70 districts in 16 states and Union Territories have recorded more than 50 point decline in the child sex ratio. The sex ratio is lowest in Kurukshetra (Haryana), Ahmedabad and in South Delhi. Some of the most prosperous district of Punjab, Haryana, Gujarat and Himachal Pradesh have the lowest sex ratios. Besides the decline between 1991-2001 has been recorded in all districts of Punjab and all district have a sex ratio of below 850 (2001). A similar trend has been recorded in Haryana, Gujarat and Delhi.

Besides, aborting female fetuses is common among upper-middle class educated couples.

In spite of the Passage of Regulation and Prevention of Misuse of PDI (pre-natal diagnostic Investigation Technology) in 1994, in 2001 the child sex ratio (0-6 age group) has declined from 945 to 927. Death rate by sex among 0-4 age group is 24.8 for girls and 22.7 for boys (Gopalan Table 4.4 page 74). However, over-all sex ratio has gone up somewhat between 1991-2001 primarily due to longer expectation of life for women than men. Better outreach of health facilities (the per capita expenditure on health has gone up from Rs. 0.61 in 1951 to Rs. 85.10 in 1994-1995 (Gopalan Table 4.9 page 125). Intensive healthcare awareness programmes run by the government and the

NGOs have contributed to better health so has use of soap and more availability of water.

However, increase in sex ratio between 1991-2001 is primarily due to higher life expectancy of women. Programme for awareness on family planning and late marriage have led to decline in fertility rates from 5.3 (1970) to 3.4 (1991).

Gender Equality, Women's movement and Women's Empowerment

The women's movement in India today is a rich and vibrant movement, which has spread to various parts of the country. Women's movement consists of female-headed NGOs working for welfare of women who became activists and raised the issue of social, economic, legal and political discrimination suffered by Indian women who because of the patriarchal structures of the society were far from equal with men. During the last thirty years the movement has gone through a process of maturing from a demand and demonstration phase to mature intervention in policy, active participation in creating new institutional and organizational structures, professionalism and participation in discussions at local, national and international levels. The issue taken up by the movement are located within the sphere of the private, and are directly linked to the body and a woman's position within the family while understanding fully that what happens within the four walls of the house has direct correlation with what is happening outside of it and that public and private are connected and what happens inside the home is the result of patriarchy which pervades all institutions - private and public.

Since women are not equal to men, there is need to fight the current social attitudes and change institutional frame works that stand in the way of equality. The efforts will have to be made at two levels: one to trigger the process of equity and second to empower women through awareness generation on their current situation and their rights, with particular focus on grass root women. They held demonstration, and public campaign and used theatre as a median for awareness generation.

The seventies consisted of various scattered movements that addressed issues ranging from the creation of the Self Employed Women's Association (SEWA) and their struggle for equal wages to the Chipko movement's effort to raise the issue of a woman's right to land. Towards the end of the 1970s and the beginning of 1980s there was enormous increase in establishment of various women's groups, many registering themselves as NGOs in order to be able to collect funds for their activities.

In addition to earlier methods, the eighties were characterized by attempts to develop structures, coalition groups, support institutions as well as developing, global sisterhood. Women's organizations were active on a whole range of issues, which they saw were interlinked to control over women's bodies. They took up the issues of rape, domestic violence, dowry, personal law, sati and fought for the creation of new women-sensitive laws or amendments to existing laws.

The eighties began with the first National Conference on the Women's Movement that addressed the issue of rape and harrassment of women. The Mathura Rape Case in 1980 ended the silence on violence against women, which led in 1983 to an amendment in laws pertaining to rape. Among the provisions was a minimun seven years imprisonment. However, these laws still remain anti-women and ineffective and sustained advocacy efforts to amend and implement these further continues.

When it come to domestic violence women's groups were successful in their struggle to introduce a legal provision which established this as a crime which the police were obliged to register and act upon-Section 498 A under the Indian Penal Code (IPC). Under this violence inflicted on a woman by her husband or his family was declared a non-bailable, non-cognizable offence. But as has been mentioned earlier there is a steep rise in the reported crimes against women among which domestic violence incidences constitute a major form of violence and that while women do find the courage to report the cases 80% of them are dropped. Recently under pressure from the movement and its spokesperson, the National Commission for Women, the Government of India has passed a 'Protection of Women from Domestic violence Act which has given the women wide ranging rights in case of domestic violence.

In 1982 an amendment was passed to the Dowry Prohibition Act, which stated that an official inquiry would be conducted if the wife died within seven years of marriage. If found guilty of dowry harassment the husband (and co-accused) faced seven years in jail as well as fines. Some of the other important decisions taken were those surrounding stree dhan (the gifts given to the bride by her parents, husband and in-laws).

Personal law was addressed in 1985 with the Shahbano case. It raised the issue of divorce (talaaq) and maintenance of Muslim women. Despite official roadblocks the Supreme Court gave a landmark ruling. It established the right of a Muslim woman to maintenance. However, the Government of India bowed down to religious sentiments against interference in the personal laws of Muslims.

In the early campaigns, groups learnt from day to day that targeting the State was not enough and that victims also needed support. So a further level of work was needed: awareness raising or conscientization so that violence against women could be prevented, rather than only dealt with after it had happened. Legal aid and counseling centers were set up, and attempts were made to establish women's shelters.

It was only when groups began to feel sucked into the overwhelming volume of the day-to-day work of such centers that they began to feel that it was not enough to do what they now saw as 'reformist' and 'non-campaign' work. Knowledge was recognized as an important need. India is such a vast country; what did activists in Karnataka, a state in southern India, know of what was going on in Garhwal in north India? And yet, everywhere you looked, there was women's activity, activity that could not necessarily be defined as 'feminist', but that was, nonetheless, geared towards improving the conditions of women's lives.

In the nineties women took up the issue of communalism and globalisation and feminisation of poverty through wider networking both at the national and international level. As the movement moved from women's issues to issues of livelihood and sustainable development they began to addres the issue of population policy demanding the exclusion e.g. of Norplant in the Family Planning Programme because of its devastating side effects, taking forward the campaign against hazardous contraceptive technologies started in the eighties. The politics of population growth and control was further brought out at the international level in the 1994 UN International Conference on Population and Development.

The movement has realized that unless women have access to elected offices, even democracies will simply be masking another kind of dictatorship – the imposition of male agendas over female ones. In view of the current patriarchal structures, however, the only way women can enter the sphere of elected political offices is through reservation of seats for women. Earlier the 73rd and 74 Amendment to the Constitution mandated 33.3% of seats for women in Panchayati Raj Institutions and urban local bodies. The women's groups are demanding some reservation in state legislatures and in the national Parliament.

The increasing feminization of poverty and violence against women emerge as the two main concerns at the Beijing Conference of delegates.

Strategies for Women's Empowerment used by the feminist groups is reformist and therefore techniques use are advocacy, lobbying, litigation, and monitoring; they use any technique that has promise and they change tactics if necessary. The favored techniques have been, Protest, Litigation, Lobbying and monitoring.

Feminists have been able to rely on preexisting structure of traditional women's groups (AICC, YWCA, NFIW, AIDWA, MDS etc) whose shared interests in many feminists issues has produced numbers and assistance that would otehrwise have been costly and probably unattainable. Women's reservation Bill, The dowry bill and the Mathura Rape case served as a model of structure and tactics and provided considerable assistance to the incipient feminist movement as it developed. Thus despite the existence of numerous autonomous sub-groupings that compete for funding and influence, there is extensive coalition building and remarkable unity among feminists. Friendship among group activists as well as multiple group membership provide linkages and facilitate the sharing of information, mobilization of activity on a specific activity and for planning of joint strategy and ad hoc coalitions are also created as necessary within the movement and with allied groups. Thus women's movement has consciously engaged in network building and has created an effective mechanism for both specialization and cohesion. The movement is capable of energetic action through inter-group mobilization when necessary. (The amount of energy unleashed by the movement during the time of international conferences like the Fourth Women's Conference in Beijing effected partly by the huge funds invested by the united nations and several other donor agencies needs to be analyzed, however).

Organization of grassroots women into groups around an economic activity or a social issue and conscientizing the group on their rights, the effect of patriarchy and the advantages of working as groups for enhancing their economic activity has greatly empowered grass root women. Through group strength the women have been able to punish their tormentors. They have been successful in closing shops selling liquor and even in killing their tormenters within the premises of a courtroom in the presence of law enforcement authorities whom they found incapable of enforcing laws. (The Nagpur Aku Yadav case)

In spite of limitation of resources feminists have been creative in the utilization of the resources they do posses. They have exercised flexibility in choosing strategies and approaches and have employed traditional pressure-group tactics with considerable skill. The simultaneous reliance on groups' specialization and coalition activity has maximized the effective use of existing resources. To change the society in which one lives its first necessary to modify the belief system of the people living in the society - one available route is education.

Selection of Issues and Success

When issues the movement has taken over are perceived as affecting role equity rather than role change, the opportunities for favorable impact on the political system has been maximized for feminist groups. Several factors are crucial to attainment of goals: the issue should have a broad based support, the issue is narrow enough not to challenge basic values or divide supporters; a policy network with access and capability of providing information to decision makers, the willingness to compromise with constituents groups and in the political process and ability to define success in terms of increments of change rather than total victory. A major factor that influences success is the image of broad based support. Focus on role of equity has found considerable support. When more dominant values are in question and role change issues are at stake the possibility of success becomes limited. Confrontation has not been the chosen strategy. The tactics of the women's groups has been centrist. Women also compromise on their demands - as are being pressurized to do in passage of the Women's Reservation Bill.

Successful group provide informational resources to bureaucrats and members of Parliament as well as state legislatures. To this day the most detailed and comprehensive public record of discrimination has been provided by the publication of Equality Now (1975).

Present Status of the Movement

The movement has become professional zed and bureaucratized. However, the early emphasis of the movement on "sisterhood" has remained a unifying force as a result, inclusivity remains as an operating principle. The commitment has remained movement oriented negating the role of the media stars or charismatic leaders preventing organizational demise with the departure of the key individual. Feminists possess little resources but high status.

The movement has gained widespread acceptance as a legitimate pressure group.

The multiple activities and success related to equity question will keep the movement alive. In addition more laws affecting equity roles are enacted and the law protects more rights for women, sufficient momentum will be sustained to keep the movement as a viable force in politics. The movement, so far, made limited use of the courts, however if women's reservation bill fails the courts may be one avenue for redress that the movement may use to greater advantage. In the coming decade more emphasis on cementing gains already made, by continued monitoring of the commitment of administrative agencies to enforcement of existing laws. Effective impact on some issues will involve participation of women affected by it with the feminist activists.

If the women's movement continues to abide by the "political rules of the game" and if parameters are drawn around issues selected for advocacy, feminist will continue to be successful political participants in an age of declining parties and pluralist expansion of interest group politics. Today the women's movement in India is rich and vibrant, which has spread to various parts of the country.

In spite of limitation of resources feminists has been creative in the utilization of the resources they do posses. They have exercised flexibility in choosing strategies and approaches and have employed traditional pressure-group tactics with considerable skill. The simultaneous reliance on groups' specialization and coalition activity has maximized the effective use of existing resources. To change the society in which one lives its first necessary to modify the belief system of the people living in the society - one available route is education.

When issues the movement has taken over are perceived as affecting role equity rather than role change, the opportunities for favorable impact on the political system has been maximized for feminist groups. Several factors are crucial to attainment of goals; the issue should have a broad based support, it should be narrow enough not to challenge basic values or divide supporters; a policy network with access and capability of providing information to decision makers, the willingness to compromise with constituents groups and in the political process and ability to define success in terms of increments of change rather than total victory.

A major factor that influences success is the image of broad based support. Focus on role equity has found considerable support. When more dominant values are in question and role change issues are at stake the possibility of success becomes limited.

Successful groups provide informational resources to bureaucrats and members of Congress. To this day the most detailed and comprehensive public record of discrimination has been provided by the publication of Equality Now (1970) which has only recently been updated by the 'Unfinished Agenda' Women also compromise on their demand – as are being pressurized to do so in passage of the Women's Reservation Bill. Confrontation is not the chosen strategy and the tactics of the women's groups have been centrist.

The movement has become professional zed and bureauctratized. However, the early emphasis of the movement on "sisterhood" has remained a unifying force as result inclusivity remains as an operating principle. The commitment has remained movement oriented negating the role of the media stars or charismatic leaders preventing organizational demise with the departure of the key individual. Feminists possess little resources but high status.

The movement has gained widespread acceptance as a legitimate pressure group.

The multiple activities and success related to equity question will keep the movement alive. In addition more laws affecting equity roles are enacted and more rights for women are protected by the law sufficient momentum will be sustained to keep the movement on a viable force in politics. The movement, so far, made limited use of the courts, however if women's reservation bill fails the courts may be one avenue for redress that the movement may use to greater advantage. In the coming decades more emphasis on cementing gains already made, by continued monitoring of the commitment of administrative agencies to enforcement of existing laws. Effective impact on some issues will involve participation of women affected by it with the feminist activists.

If the women's movement continues to abide by the "political rules of the game" and if parameters are drawn around issues selected for advocacy, feminist will continue to be successful political participants in an age of declining parties and pluralist expansion of interest group politics.

References

National Commission for Women: Towards Equality-The Unfinished Agenda Status of Women in India - 2001.

Canadian International Develipment Agency (CIDA): Setting the Stage for the Next Century: The Federal Plan for Gender Equality, Status of Women Canada 1995.

OECD-DAC (Development Assistance Committee) Guidelines for Gender Equality and Women's Empowerment in Development Co-operation, Development Co-operation Guidelines Series.

List of Tables

Table 1: Literacy Rates – India; 1951-2001

Table 2: Number of Girls per 100 Boys in Primary and Secondary Schools 1950-1997

Table 3: Index of Growth in Enrolment of Girls in Higher Education 1970-71 & 1993-94

Table 4: Growth in Recognized Educational Institutions

Table 5: Women Representatives in Panchayati Raj Institutions (Percentage), 2002

Table 5A: Women in Panchayati Raj Institutions (1995-2001)

Table 6: Percentage of Female and Male voters casting their vote in each election in India

Table 7: Women's Representation in Parliament 1952-1998

Table 8: Declining Representation of Women in State Legislatures 1952-1997 (% of women MLAs)

Table 9: Representation of Women in the Central Council of Ministers, 1985-2005

Table 10: Number of Judges by Sex in Supreme Court / High Courts as on 2003

Table 11: Percentage of Women in Civil Services Personnel

Table 12: Work Participation Rates, 1971-1991, India
Table 13: Occupational Shift of Workers Through Decadal Census, 1971-1991
Table 14: Proportion of Woman among the Total Workers in the Organized Sector and Percentage increase 1971-1999
Table 15: Life Expectancy at Birth of males and females during the past 100 year4s
Table 16: Estimated infant mortality rates by sex and residence, India 1972-1998
Table 17: Sex ratio of Population (F/M 1000) 1901-2001

3

Women Empowerment: A Key to Development

Over the past decade, gender equality and women's empowerment have been explicitly recognized as key not only to the health of nations, but also to social and economic dement. India's National Population Policy 2000 has 'empowering women for health and nutrition as one of its crosscutting strategic themes. The promotion of gender equality and empowering of women is one of the eight Millennium Development Goals (MDG) to which India is a signatory.

The pairing of the two concepts of women's empowerment and gender equality into one MDG implicitly recognizes that gender equality and women's empowerment are two sides

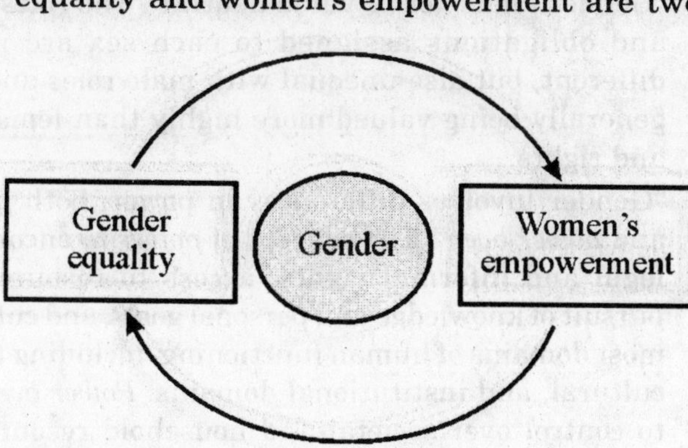

of the same coin: progress toward gender equality requires women's empowerment and women's empowerment requires increases in gender equality as shown.

Since gender inequality and women's disempowerment occur in all the different domains in which women and men interact and function, both concepts are multi-dimensional; consequently, they give rise to a large number of potential indicators. Indicators of gender equality/inequality are typically designed to compare the status of women and men on particular characteristics of interest; whereas, by definition, indicators of empowerment;' disempowerment tend not to be relative. Instead, indicators of empowerment are designed to measure roles, attitudes, and rights of women and sometimes men.

In order to measure gender equality and women's empowerment, the concerts need to be clearly defined and their hypothesized associations with each other and health outcomes discussed. In common parlance, the terms gender and sex are often used interchangeably; however, they are distinct concepts. Whereas, sex of individuals is largely determined by biology, their gender is socially constructed and comprises the roles, rights, and obligations that attach to them on the basis of their sex. Kishor (2006) identifies three important aspects of gender namely:

a) "Gender tends not be value neutral". The roles, rights, and obligations assigned to each sex are not just different, but also unequal with male roles and rights generally being valued more highly than female roles and rights.
b) "Gender involves differences in power, both *power to* and *power over*". The concept of *power to* encompasses legal and informal rights, access to resources, and pursuit of knowledge and personal goals, and cuts across most domains of human functioning, including familial, cultural, and institutional domains. *Power over* refers to control over societal and household resources and

decisions, cultural and religious ideology, and one's own and others' bodies. Importantly, men tend to have greater power than women, and, in some domains, even have power *over* women.

c) "Gender is not static or immutable". Being socially constructed, gender roles, rights, and expectations can change over time and across geographical space as societal needs, opportunities, and customs change.

As a result of (a) and (b), inequalities based on gender, as also the disempowerment of females, are pervasive in most societies, particularly patriarchal ones such as in India. Gender-based differences in power and resource-access have consequences for the quality of life of the population, including its health, as shown in the figure below.

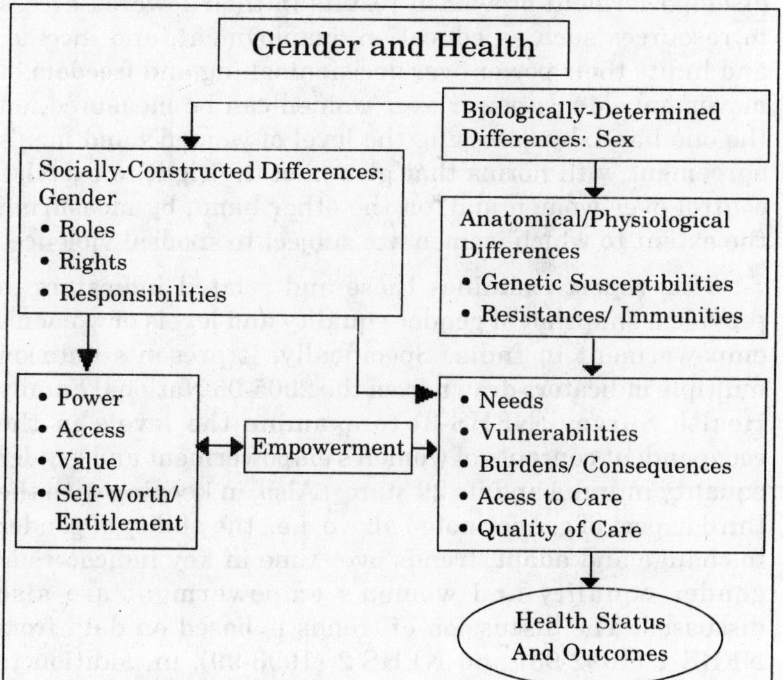

As the figure shows, gender affects health outcomes through male and female differences in roles, access, and power, and sex differentially affects the health of women and men because of biologically determined physiological and genetic differences that manifest in differences in needs and vulnerabilities. While the type of health care needed can vary by sex, whether, for example, the type of care needed can be *accessed is* affected by gender, empowerment, and sex.

Gender-based inequalities translate into greater value being placed on the health and survival of males than of females. In India, examples of health and population indicators that are driven by gender differences in the perceived worth of males and females include sex ratios at birth, infant and child mortality by sex, and low ages at marriage for women. Further, at the household level, disempowerment of women results in their lowered access to resources such as education, employment, and income, and limits their power over decisionmaking and freedom of movement. Men's power over women can be measured, on the one hand, by assessing the level of women's and men's agreement with norms that give men the right to exercise control over women and, on the other hand, by measuring the extent to which women are subject to spousal violence.

This report examines these and related indicators to provide a snapshot of gender equality and levels of women's empowerment in India. Specifically, it presents data on multiple indicators drawn from the 2005-06 National Family Health Survey (NFHS-3) to examine the levels in the codependent concepts of women's empowerment and gender equality in India and its 29 states. Also, in keeping with the third aspect of gender noted above, i.e., the ability of gender to change and adapt, trends over time in key indicators of gender equality and women's empowerment are also discussed. The discussion of trends is based on data from NFHS-1 (1992-93) and NFHS-2 (1998-99), in addition to NFHS-3 data. The report also examines the determinants of specified indicators and their linkages to selected health and nutritional outcomes.

In addition to this chapter, the report has 11 other chapters. Each of the first nine of these chapters is organized around a set of related indicators of gender equality and/or women's empowerment. Chapter 11 examines gender differences in children's immunization and child and adult nutrition, and shows how these indicators and women's contraceptive use are related to selected indicators of women's empowerment. Chapter 12 presents some conclusions. At the end of most chapters, appendix tables show key indicators discussed in the chapter by state and for the eight cities for which representative indicators can be estimated. The indicators for these cities are also provided separately for the slum and nonslum areas in these eight cities.

The information in this report should be treated as complementary to the gender-related information in Volume 1 of the NFHS-3 National Report, especially in its Chapters 14 and 15. A fundamental indicator of gender inequality in India, and arguably; one of the most powerful, is a preference

Figure 3.1 Trends in the sex ratio (females per 1,000 males) of the defacto population age 0-6 year, India

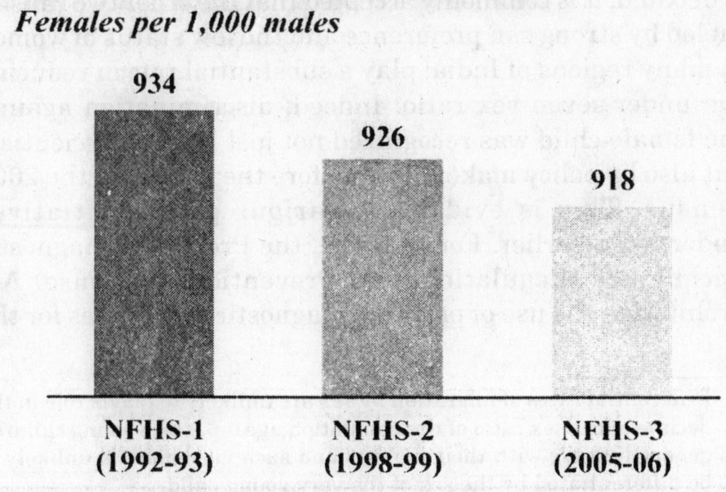

for sons so strong that it is manifested as limiting the birth and survival of girls. The 2001 census data for India revealed a sharp, decline in the sex ratio for the population age 0-6; from 945 females in 1991 to 927 females per 1,000 males. The trend in the sex ratio of the under-seven population based on National Family Health Survey data for the period 1992-93 to 2005-06 also provides evidence of continued decline and shows that in 2005-06 the under-seem sex ratio had fallen further to 918 females per 1,000 males (Figure 3.1).

The decline over time in the under-seven sex ratio can have one or more of mainly three possible causes: a decrease in the sex ratio at birth through the use of technologies that enable sex selection, an increase in the mortality of girl children compared with the mortality of boy children, suggesting intensification of the already documented discrimination against the girl child (Miller; 1981; Das Gupta, 1987; Kishor, 1993); or a systematic: undercount of female children, compared with male children under the age of seven[1].

Even as the role, if any, of the last of these possible causes is debated, it is commonly accepted that the other two causes, fueled by strong son preference and the low status of women in many regions of India; play a substantial role in reducing the under-seven sex ratio. Indeed, discrimination against the female child was recognized not just by social scientists but also by policy makers long before the release of the 2001 Census. This is evident in various policy initiatives undertaken earlier. For example, the Pre-Natal Diagnostic Techniques (Regulation. and Prevention of Misuse) Act prohibiting the use of prenatal diagnostic techniques for the

1. Differential rates of migration by sex are unlikely to play a role in the decline of the sex ratio of the population age 0-6, since young children generally move with their parents and such movement is unlikely to be differentiated by the sex of the very young child.

purpose of prenatal sex determination was passed as early as 1994 in recognition of the widespread use of ultrasound and related technologies to eliminate unwanted female foetuses Further, the National Population Policy of 2000 explicitly recognized the problem and suggested policy initiatives directed toward ending discriminatory practices that adversely affect the health of the girl child (Ministry of Health and Family Welfare, 2000).

Since the pathways to a lower sex ratio of the population age 0-6 mainly involve a low sex ratio at birth and/or excess female mortality after birth, this chapter examines the levels of these and related indicators, including the sex ratio of live births by whether the mother had an ultrasound test during pregnancy. The chapter focuses on the sex ratio at birth, providing insight into how this ratio varies for all births and last births.

The overall sex ratio at birth can be directly affected by the use of modern technologies that allow couples to have only children of a desired sex[2]. In addition, where strong couple-level gender preferences exist, couples are more likely to stop having children only when their desired sex combination of children has been achieved. This 'stopping' behaviour will not affect the overall sex ratio at birth, but will affect the sex ratios at birth of last births. For example, in societies with strong son preference, last births are more likely to be male, and females are more likely to grow up in large families. Thus, an examination of sex ratios of last births provides insight into the pervasiveness of son preference.

---

2. Such technologies include ultrasound and amniocentesis tests, which can routinely reveal the sex of a foetus. A foetus of an unwanted sex can then be aborted. Other, even more advanced technologies, such as sperm-sorting techniques, can select the sex of the child before conception; these techniques are less comonly available in India, however.

Sex Ratios at Birth

The sex ratio at birth is defined as the number of live female births per 1,000 live male births. A fall in this ratio implies that the number of females born alive is declining relative to the number of males born alive. In evaluating sex ratios in terms of relative female or male deficits at birth, the relevant comparator is not equality in the number of females and males (i.e., a sex ratio of 1,000), however. This is because in most populations more males than females are born (Waldron, 1983; 1998). The sex ratio at birth recorded across most developing countries has been found to vary in a narrow range from 943 to 971 (United Nations Development Programme, 1998).

Figure 3.2 Trends in the sex ratios at birth for all children born in the five complete calendar years preceding NFHS-1, NFHS-2, and NFHS-3, India

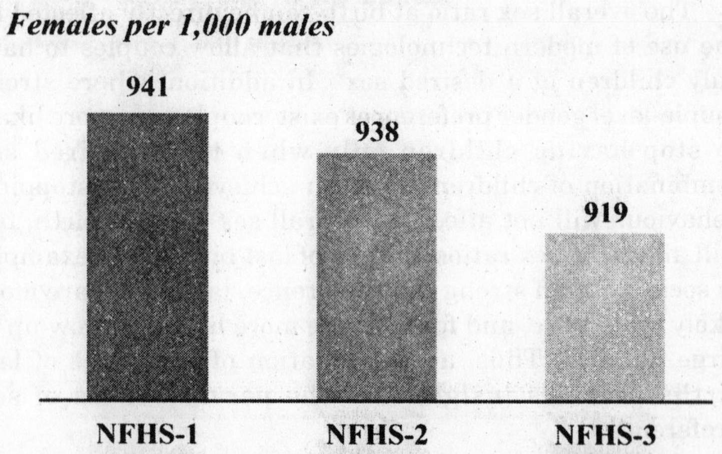

Levels and trends in the sex ratio at birth In India, the sex ratio at birth calculated for all births in the five complete calendar-year periods before each of the three National Family Health Surveys not only shows a downward trend in the sex ratio at birth in the six years between 1987-91 and

1993-97, but also shows an acceleration in the decline in the sex ratio between 1993-97 and 2000-04 (Figure 3.2). In the late 1980s and early 1990s, the sex ratios at birth at 941 and 938 respectively, did not deviate too far from 943, which

Figure 3.3 Trends in the sex ratios at birth of live births and births that have died in the five complete calendar-years preceding NFHS-1, NFHS-2, and NFHS-3, India

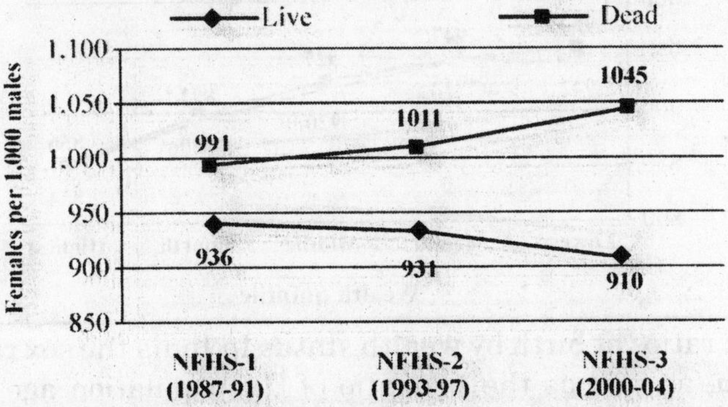

is the lowest sex ratio at birth within the normal range. However, by the early 2000s the sex ratio at birth in India had fallen well below the normal range to 919.

After birth, genetic vulnerabilities result in higher male than female mortality during early childhood in most populations, especially at the neonatal stage. An examination of the trends in the sex ratios at birth by the survival status of the child in the five complete calendar-year periods before each of the three NFHS surveys, however, reveals a strong female disadvantage in survival (Figure 3.3).

The sex ratio of births that died in each of the five calendar-year periods increased from 991 females per 1,000 males in the period 1987-91 to 1,045 females in the period 2000-04. In the same time period, the sex ratio of surviving births declined from 936 to 910. (Notably, the sex ratio at birth of surviving births closely mirrors the sex ratio at birth for all births, since births that survive constitute a large majority of all births.) These data suggest that not only are fewer than expected females being born, but females are increasingly over-represented in births that die.

Figure 3.4 Sex ratio of population Age 0-6 years and sex ratio at birth for all births to women age 15-49 is five

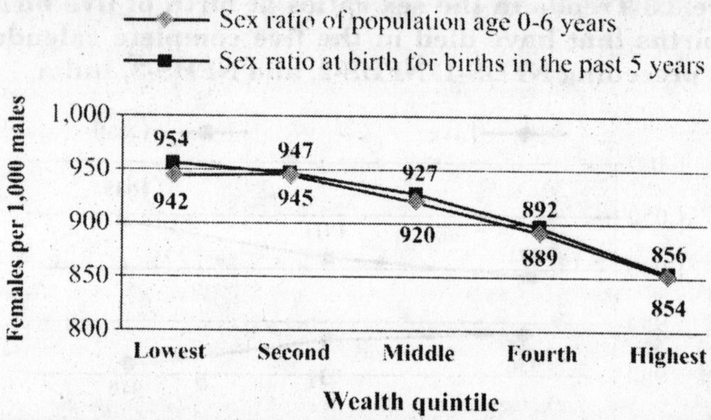

Sex ratios at birth by wealth status In India the sex ratio at birth, as well as the sex ratio of the population age 0-6 years, varies greatly by household wealth status. In fact, the sex ratio at birth in the five years preceding NFHS-3 is highest, at 954 females per 1,000 males, in the lowest wealth quintile (Figure 3.4). The sex ratio at birth for births to women in the second wealth quintile, though slightly lower, is also within the normal range for sex ratios at birth (943-971). Beyond the second wealth quintile, however, the sex ratio at birth falls dramatically by wealth to a low of 854 for births to women in the highest quintile. As expected, the sex ratio of the population age 0-6, which captures the sex ratio of surviving births, also follows a similar pattern.

Sex ratios at birth by use of ultrasound testing during pregnancy Sex ratios at birth can diverge greatly from the normal range only with the use of technologies that can help choose or determine the sex of the foetus, such as ultrasound diagnostic testing during pregnancy. In India, 24% of all pregnancies in the five years preceding NFHS-3 received an ultrasound test (IIPS and Macro International,

2007). NFHS-3 shows that it is pregnancies to women in the highest wealth quintile that are most likely to receive an ultrasound test: the proportion of pregnancies receiving an ultrasound test increases from only 4% and 10% for pregnancies to women in the lowest and the second wealth quintile to 21% and 38% for pregnancies in the next two quintiles, and finally to a high of 62% in the highest wealth quintile. While a substantial proportion of ultrasound tests are done for diagnostic purposes, an examination of sex ratios at birth can reveal the extent to which ultrasound testing is being used for sex selection.

In India, sex ratios at birth estimated separately for pregnancies with and without ultrasound testing provide clear evidence that many, women are using ultrasound tests for sex selection. The sex ratio at birth for completed pregnancies in the five years preceding NFHS-3 with an ultrasound test during pregnancy is only 851, compared with 941 for completed pregnancies with no ultrasound test. Thus, pregnancies with an ultrasound test have a sex ratio at birth that is much lower than the biologically normal sex ratio, while those with no test have a sex ratio that is close to the normal.

Figure 3.5 Sex ratios of completed pregnancies in the five year preceding NFHS-3 with and without an ultrasound test by wealth quintile, NFHS-3, India

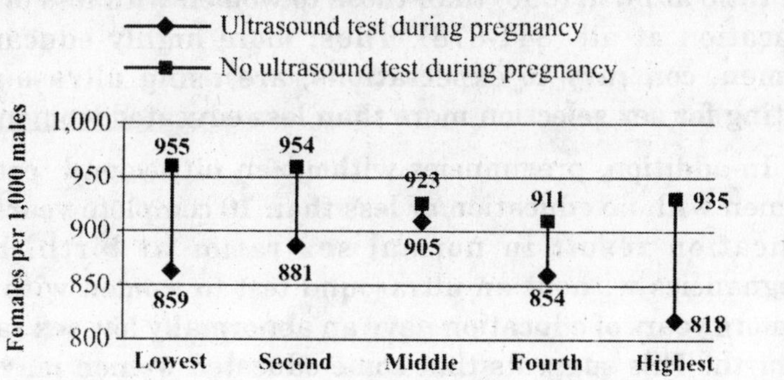

The much lower sex ratios at birth at each level of wealth for completed pregnancies that had an ultrasound test, compared with those that did not, provide evidence that ultrasound tests are often being used for the purpose of sex selection at all levels of wealth. Figure 2.5 also shows that the sex ratio of completed pregnancies with an ul-trasound test to women in the highest wealth quintile (818) is much lower than for pregnancies with an ultrasound to women in any other wealth quintile (854-905). This suggests that women in the highest wealth quintile are more likely than women in the lower wealth quintiles to be using ultrasound tests for sex selection.

It could be argued that while wealth may only help to increase access to sex-selection technology, education has the additional potential to inform and empower women in ways that can reduce son preference. NFHS-3 shows that use of ultrasound tests increases with women's education: For pregnancies in the five years prior to NFHS-3, 9% had an ultrasound test if the mother had no education, compared with 58% if the mother had 10 or more years of education.

Figure 3.6 shows that pregnancies with an ultrasound test have an abnormally low sex ratio at birth irrespective of mother's level of education. Further, pregnancies to women with 10 or more years of education have a somewhat lower sex ratio at birth (830) than those to women with less or no education at all (841-878). Thus, more highly educated women, contrary to expectations, are using ultrasound testing for sex selection more than less educated women.

In addition, pregnancies without an ultrasound test to women with no education or less than 10 complete years of education result in normal sex ratios at birth, but pregnancies without an ultrasound test to women with 10 or more years of education have an abnormally low sex ratio at birth. This suggests that some educated women may be using sex-selection methods that are not being reported.

Figure 3.6 Sex ratios of completed pregnancies in the five years preceding NFHS-3 with and without an ultrasound test by mother's education, NFHS-3, India

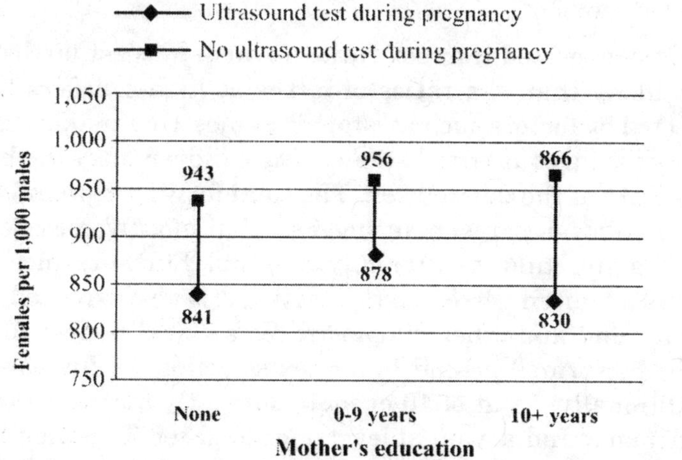

Overall, these data show that more educated women are having disproportionately more sons than daughters, both in absolute terms and compared with women in other educational groups.

Sex ratios et birth by birth order The sex ratio at birth for a population is a single number, an average for all births in a given time period. This ratio does not differentiate between sex ratios at birth for births with different characteristics or for births tc couples with different fertility-related desires. This section explores how sex ratios at birth vary by birth order.

If son preference exists in a society, evidence of it will typically be found in lower sex ratios at lower birth orders relative to those at higher birth orders and for last births compared with all other births. A caveat regarding a potential source of error is necessary here since this analysis is based on all children ever born (i.e., all births in the survey and not just recent births) to women in the age range of 15-

49. Recall error tends to increase the further back in time one goes. The sex ratio at birth will be affected if there is any tendency to recall births of one sex more than births of another sex.

It is expected that sex ratios at birth for first births are less likely than sex ratios of births at higher orders to be affected by factors such as 'stopping rules' that make it more likely that a couple will stop having children after the birth of a child of the desired sex. The total fertility rate in India of 2.7 children per woman suggests that most women do not stop having children after only one child. Further, since first births are often perceived to be risky, it is also expected that ultrasound and other diagnostic tests would be less likely, to be performed primarily for sex selection for first births. Additionally, 7 out of 10 or more currently married women and men in India want at least one daughter. Together these factors suggest that the sex of the first child is less likely to be controlled.

Despite expectations to the contrary, Table 3.1 shows that the sex ratio at birth for first-born children has been below normal in all three NFHS surveys and has been declining steadily since NFHS-1. This is also true for births

Table 3.1 Trends in sex ratios at birth (females per 1,000 males) by birth order of all births to women age 15-49, India

	NFHS-1	NFHS-2	NFHS-3
Birth order			
1	901	873	843
2	819	765	762
3	832	819	837
4	921	919	961
5	986	1,019	1,026
6	1,002	1,052	1,054
7+	1,039	1,034	1,094
Total	935	920	926

at birth order two. However, in all three surveys, the sex ratio at birth for births at order two is substantially lower than at order one and at any other birth order. The sex ratio at birth for births at order three is also lower than the sex ratio at birth for all births except births at order two. This suggests that substantial proportions of couples with two or three children stop having more children if their last birth is a boy and this has been happening since the early 1990s at the time of NFHS-1. Stopping after two or three children is in keeping with the mean ideal family size of currently married women in India, which has been between 2 and 3 children in all three surveys.

Sex ratios at birth (females per 1,000 males) for all births in the five years preceding the survey, NFHS-3, India

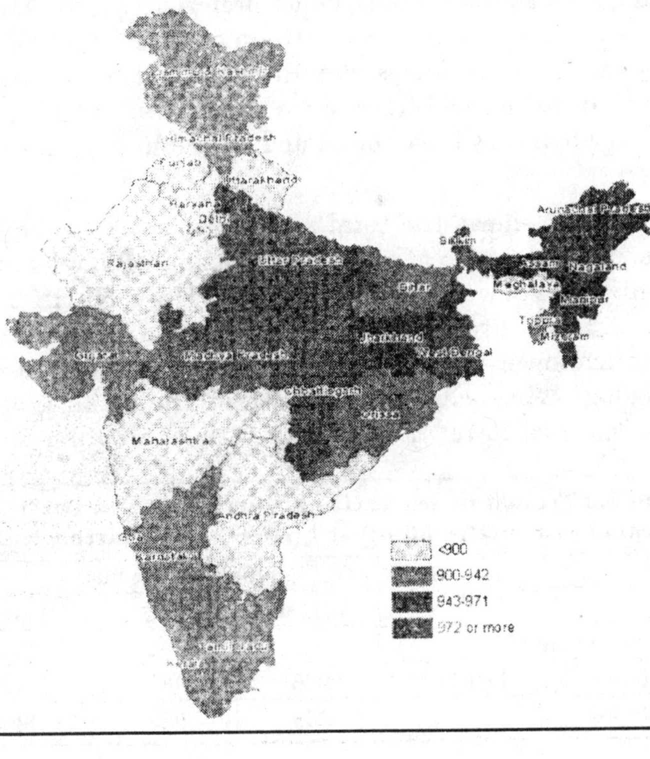

Sex ratios at birth by state The sex ratio at birth by state ranges from a low of 728 in Punjab and 756 in Haryana to a high of 1,102 in Jharkhand (Appendix 2).

There are only five states–Chhattisgarh, Madhya Pradesh, Uttar Pradesh, West Bengal, and Nagaland-where the sex ratio at birth lies in the normal range (943-971) and six states where it lies above the normal range. Of the six states with higher than normal sex ratios at birth, all except Jharkhand are in the northeast of the country.

Thus, in 18 of the 29 states in India the sex ratio at birth is below normal. Notably, all four of the southern states, including Kerala, have lower than normal sex ratios at birth.

Sex Ratios at Birth of Last Births

Yet another way to examine gender preferences is to examine sex ratios at birth of last births. If son preference is affecting family-building strategies, sex ratios of last births will be lower than for other births since couples will stop having children when they have completed their family with a birth of a son.

Table 3.2 shows the total sex ratios, sex ratios of last births, and sex ratios of all other births for all births in the birth histories of women age 15-49 in NFHS-1, NFHS-2, and NFHS-3. In all three surveys, the sex ratio of last births has been much lower than that for all births and the disparity has been growing over time. In NFHS-1, the sex ratio of last births was 14% lower than the sex ratio of all other births;

Table 3.2 Trends in sex ratios at birth (females per 1,000 males) of last births, all other births, and all births, India

	Sex ratio at birth		
	NFHS-1	NFHS-2	NFHS-3
Last births only	837	791	756
All births except last births	976	981	1,016
All births	935	920	926

this disparity increased to 19% in NFHS-2 and then to 26% in NFHS-3. Thus, sex ratios of last births favour boys much more now than they did in the early 1990s. Strong son preference also suggests that if a birth results in a female child then it is not likely to be a last birth. Thus, the fact that the sex ratios of all births other than last births are predominantly female is well in keeping with son preference. The increase over time in the proportion of females in the sex ratio of births that are not last births suggests that now, even more than before, female births are less likely to be last births.

Sex ratios of last births by women's contraceptive use Because birth histories are collected from women who are at different points in their family formation process, some of the births considered to be last births will not in fact be 'last'. One way to refine this analysis is to look at sex ratios of last births to women by their current use of contraception. Of particular importance in this context is the adoption of sterilization, since sterilization signifies the end of childbearing. Notably, at the time of NFHS-3, sterilization accounted for more than two-thirds of current contraceptive use in India.

Figure 3.7 Trends in sex ratios at birth for last births by mother's current use of contraception

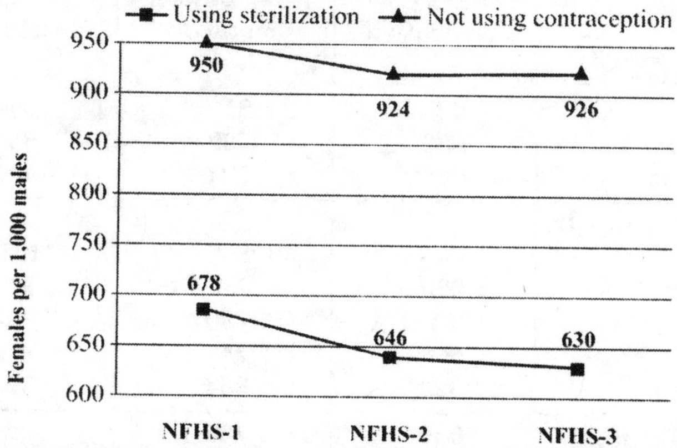

The sex ratio at birth of last births to women who are sterilized, at 630, is much lower than for last births to women who are not using any method of contraception (926). It is also lower, as expected, than the sex ratio for all last births (756), which include some births to women who are planning to have more children. Notably, too, the sex ratio of last births to even women using a temporary method of contraception is much lower than normal. Sex ratios at birth of last births were in the 600s for sterilized women even in NFHS-1; but as Figure 3.7 shows, they have fallen somewhat over time from 678 at the time of NFHS-1 to 630 in NFHS-3. Also notable is that the sex ratio at birth of last births to women who are not using any contraception fell from a normal level in NFHS-l to below normal in NFHS-2 and has changed little since then.

Table 3.3 shows that for sterilized women, the sex ratios of last births are in the 600s, irrespective of wealth status or mothers' education. Further, the sex ratio of last births declines sharply with wealth and mothers' education even

Table 3.3 Sex ratios at birth of last births by current contraceptive use according to mother's education and wealth quintile, NFHS-3, India.

	Type of contraception being used		
	Sterilization	Any other method	No method
Education			
None	625	818	950
0-9 years	632	739	652
10+ years	645	634	640
Wealth quintile			
Lowest	644	869	1017
Second	620	788	960
Middle	64	780	903
Fourth	600	745	872
Highest	629	654	822
Total	**630**	**735**	**926**

among women who are not using any contraception although it is in the normal or above-normal range for women with no education and women belong-ing to the lowest two wealth quintiles. For women using a method other than sterilization, the sex ratio of last births also declines sharply with education and wealth, but is never above normal in any education or wealth category.

Thus, the sex ratio at birth for last births to women using any method of contraception are below normal, irrespective of the method or the education or wealth category to which the women belong.

Sex ratios of last births by state The sex ratio of last births is below normal in all states of India except Kerala

Sex ratios at birth (females per 1,000 males) for all last births to women age 15-49 years, NFHS-3, India

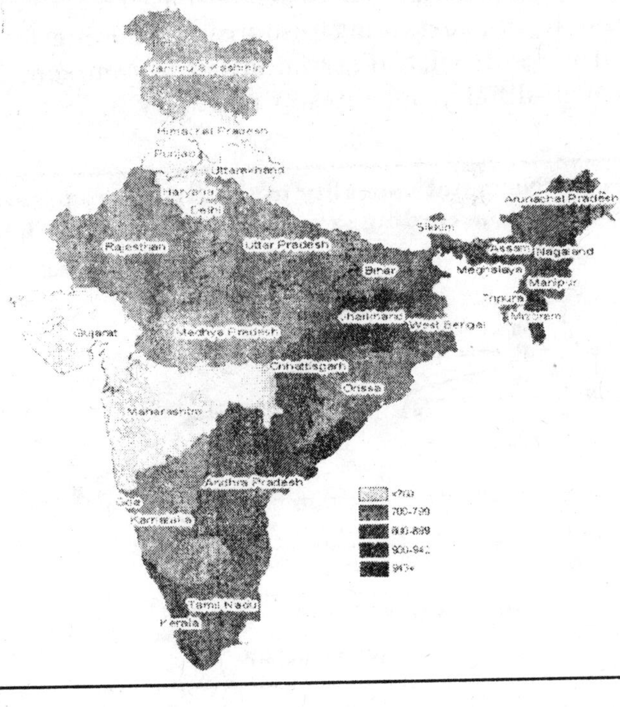

and Mizoram. The sex ratio of last births ranges from a low of 504 in Punjab, 540 in Haryana, and 572 in Himachal Pradesh, to a high of 944 in Mizoram and 973 in Kerala. The only other state where the sex ratio of last births is anywhere close to normal is Nagaland (see Appendix 2). These very low sex ratios of last births in most states of India suggest that son preference is continuing to influence fertility decisions in most of India.

Sex Differentials in Mortality

Sex ratios at birth measure gender inequality in terms of the extent to which the number of female births relative to male births deviates from biological expectations and focus attention on whether girls are being discriminated against regarding their right to birth. However, what about the girls that are born? Does son preference differentially affect girls' survival by subjecting them to gender-based discrimination in access to life-sustaining resources, including food and medical care? If such discrimination is common, it will manifest in differential rates of mortality by sex at early ages.

Figure 3.8 Neonatal mortality in the five years preceding NFHS-3 by sex, according to wealth quintile, NFHS-3, India

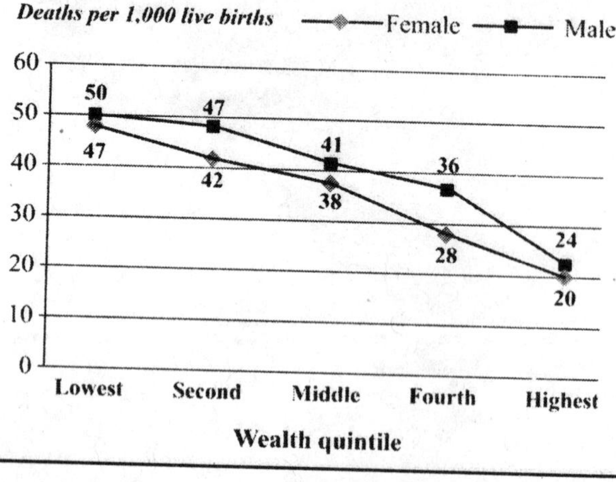

On biological grounds, mortality in infancy should be higher for male infants than female infants particularly in the first month of life. In accordance with this expectation, NFHS-3 shows that the neonatal mortality rate (the number of deaths to children age less than one month per 1,000 live births) in India was 41 for males, compared with 37 for females per 1,000 births in the five years preceding the survey. Further, as Figure 3.8 shows, male neonatal mortality is higher than female neonatal mor-tality for births in all wealth quintiles.

Excess female mortality becomes evident in India in the period beyond one month of life. In most countries where infant and child mortality is driven by biology alone, female mortahty in the first year of life beyond the first month continues to be lower than male mortality. In India, however, the postneonatal mortality rate (the number of deaths to children age 1-11 months per 1,000 live births) for females is 21, compared with only 15 for boys. Further, as shown in Figure 3.9, although the female-male differential in postneonatal mortality is lowest for children born to mothers in the highest wealth quintile, the female disadvantage is, nonetheless, evident in all wealth quintiles.

Figure 3.9 Postneonatal mortality in the five years preceding NFHS-3 by sex, according to wealth quintile, NFHS-3, India

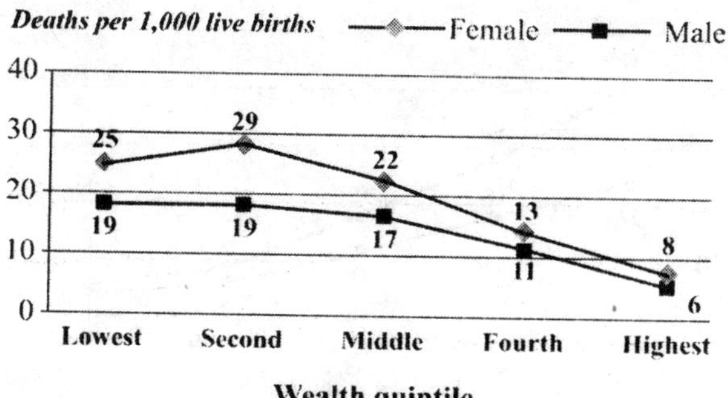

A similar pattern in gender differentials is also observed in the child mortality rate (the number of deaths to children age 1-4 years per 1,000 children reaching age 1 year). In India as a whole, the child mortal-ity rate for girls, at 23 per 1,000, is 61% higher than for boys, at 14 per 1,000.

As shown in Figure 3.10, female child mortality is higher than male child mortality in every wealth quintile. However, female child mortality drops more sharply with wealth than does male child mortality. As a consequence, the gender gap in child mortality is virtually nonexistent in the highest wealth quintile.

Thus, although Wealthier households have a lower sex ratio at birth than poorer households, the data on mortality yield two conclusions: a) girls born in wealthier households are more likely to survive their early childhood than girls born in poorer households; and b) the gender differential in survival is lower in wealthier households than in poorer households. Thus, girls born in poorer households have a much higher probability of dying than boys in poorer households; by contrast, in the wealthiest households, the probability of dying is fairly similar for both boys and girls.

Figure 3.10 Child mortality in the five years preceding NFHS-3 by sex, acording to wealth quintile, NFHS-3, India

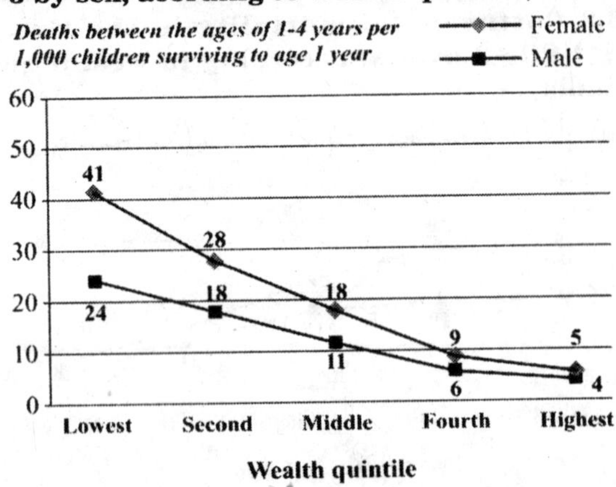

4

Women's Empowerment for Sustainable Agriculture Development

In a stratified society like ours access and empowerment of different section of the societies are becoming serious concerns and to address it planners, managers, social scientist all over the world have started deliberating and devising way out like anything. In this direction genders issues are dominating over other vulnerable issues like poverty, class conflicts, communities, ethnic issues etc. In ensuring an egalitarian development gender equity still remains as a pertinent question as it has been for the thousands of years of human civilization.

Gender issues beyond its epistemological meaning certainly imbibes other components like production relation, access to education, geographical distribution, occupational imperatives, marital system and even physical & physiological weaknesses.

The present deliberation will go contextual with the realm of women's empowerment in sustainable agriculture development. The sustainability of agriculture development has become a prerogatives to the women's participation moving across the caste, Creed and economic echelons. Our need is to ascertain and assure the areas where women are still far from enjoying the minimum privileges and question of empowerment has been thrown to a very complex, integrated situation the access to resources, institution, decision making process and information etc. are the pertinent question in making the women empowered, confident, and accorded to the mainstream social processes.

So, a stepwise discussion will unveil the areas of concerns and the expected redressals therewith:

Following are some of the major handicaps in overall development of women and the suggestions to overcome with special reference to agriculture.

Limited access to resources (Land)

Access to assets is the single most urgent need for the upliftment of women in general and farm women in particular. Though the Indian legislation permits equal right of man & women in property yet the condition in actual sense is not so. Rural women still do not have ownership on land and the pattas are allotted in the name of their husband. Due to this the cannot take independent decision on various agricultural aspects. Therefore, concerted efforts are needed to promote women access to resources. For this, following measures are suggested.

In the distribution of land to the landless women should also be included in the existing Govt. policies on distribution of joint pattas to husband & wife. Short term operational ownership of land female farmers while giving land on leasing my be arranged.

Limited access to input & credit:

Though women make substantial contributors to agriculture development, their access to the most crucial input "credit" is limited. Since they are not land owners, the credit flow generally goes in the name of male members (i.e. owners). For promoting women's access to farm input & credit. following measures may be taken:

- Credit flow to rural women could be channeled through credit & thrift societies.
- Voluntary agencies in each district may be identified which could help in developing women organizations.
- Credit organizations should simplify the procedures & modalities to suit the educational level of rural women & also organize credit camps in village exclusively for women.
- Farm women should also be recipient of credit for which possession of assets may not be insisted upon.
- Existing loaning policies of NABARD need orientation towards women credit eligibility by granting them the status of a producer.

Inadequate technical competency

Though women are involved in almost all agricultural operations, yet, they have inadequate technical competency due to their limited exposure to outside world. This has compelled them to follow the age old practices which in turn result in poor work efficiency and drudgery.

Training is an important component of HRD which enhances knowledge, skill and attitude. For building technical competency among farm women, specialized need based and skill oriented training should be organized preferably at village level. Some of the priority areas in which women need training are:

- Conservation and management of natural resources
- IPM and INM
- Renewable energy sources
- Seed production technology
- Use of fertilizer
- Post-harvest management

Looking into the importance of conservation and management of natural resources for sustainable development, due emphasis should be given on this aspect and it should be included as an essential feature in all the training programmes organized for farm women. For effective training programmes, following points should be considered.

i) Extension agencies should pursue the family approach to training

ii) Training should be organized at appropriate time specially the pre-seasonal training.

iii) There should be proper followed-up of the programmes and there should be synchronization in time between knowledge and skill transfer and the supply credit and other inputs needed to apply the knowledge.

iv) During training, the training institute should identify the active participants and intensive training should be imparted to them so that they can be used as a 'para-extension workers' for dissemination of technical information.

Poor participation in decision making

Generally, decision regarding the activities requiring technical competency and money related matters were taken by male members. Since knowledge and economic independence are the parameters of women empowerment enhancing the technical knowledge, skills and building greater involvement in various farm activities.

Poor existing Research and Extension System No or Poor gender consideration:

Though several technological breakthrough have been observed in the recent past the technologies by the researchers are not tailored to the specific needs of the farm women. With the result, most of the agricultural operations are performed manually and in an unskilled manner which results into greater drudgery on the part of farm women. In order to cater to the technological needs of the farm women, there is need to re-orient the entire research system for which following measures may be taken.

- In order to make scientific information in agriculture and skill areas more useful, it should be tested and refined keeping in view the different farming situations in socio-cultural milieu. It would lead to women specific technologies.
- Some of the tasks and operations which women are specifically involved and which are drudgery prone include transplanting, weeding, harvesting, threshing, winnowing etc. Therefore, these require special attention of the farm scientist for evolving relevant technologies or modifying the existing ones.
- The design, development and testing of agricultural implements and machinery should be undertaken with the active participation of rural women. In this regard with local artisans will he helpful. In essence machinery should be a blessing rather than become a curse.
- While evolving agricultural technologies; indigenous, practices used by women. should be paid due attention-for blending with the frontier ones for greater adoption.

Like research, existing extension systems are also not much oriented towards women folk as reflected by the fact out of the total 88,000 VEWs only about 10% (9000) are female. This has adversely affected the transfer of technology. Most of the extension programmes are "target oriented" rather than "need based" which are formulated without analysing and documenting needs of the farm women. Farm women in India have to be tackled with different kind of extension models because of the fact that they differ with men on various counts, viz. Inovativeness educational level, intellectual ability, flexibility, decision making etc. with this assumption a separate extension strategy needs to be developed for all developmental programmes intended to benefit farm women. Some of the suggestions in this ragard are:

- Women farmers should be included as the direct clientele in the existing extension systems.

- Women development projects should use participatory approach at all stages i.e. in identification of need, implementation, monitoring and evaluation.
- Under T&V system like Kisan Mandal Mahila Kisan Mandals should be constituted or at least 50% of the women participation in such groups should assured.
- In order to provide effective base for access to service and facilities, women agriculturist should be organised into autonomous groups.
- With a view to abreast women with latest agricultural innovations state govt. should initiate: "Advance Information Centre for Women" at village level.
- In order to develop and disseminate appropriate technologies for farm women, there is need to strengthen linkage between various research and extension organisations engaged in transfer of technology.
- Female extension personnel should be recruited at various hierarchical levels.

Limited exposure to mass media:

The transfer of technology approach which mainly includes mass media are also not paying due attention towards dissemination of adequate and timely agricultural information to the farm women. Some of the important points in this regards are

- At present coverage of agricultural programmes on Doordarshan is only 12% of the total telecast time (in Hindi), out of which, the programmes related to women are negligible. Therefore there is utmost need to provide adequate coverage to the programmes related to women, the authorities of mass media may apportion at least 25-30% time to farm technologies/information pin pointed to farm women.
- A few programmes which are meant for women are telecast at a time, which is not suitable for them. Therefore, the media personnel are required to pay due attention towards timings of the programmes.

- Though the broadcast of agricultural programmes on AIR is a regular feature, the programmes are monotonous in nature and stereotype. Therefore authorities of AIR should have effective linkage with communication personnel for bringing about the programmes in a variety of ways, vie. use of success stories, experience features etc. that would be more interesting to the listeners.
- Looking at the low literacy rate of rural women, technical literature developed for them should be in a simple language (preferably in local dialect) with due emphasis on illustrations so that even the neo-literates can make use of it.
- There should be state level co-ordination committee in order to review, monitor and evaluate various programmes being telecast, broadcast and published by the different print media. Feed back and suggestions of the audience/listeners/readers would improve the quality of programmes.

Untapped women potential:

Though women have many inherent capacities like high determination, sense of responsibility, better managerial ability, yet their potential has not been identified by the extension personnel. For example, women are considered as reservoirs of rich traditional wisdom with respect to various agricultural practices. This potential could be explored by the extension scientists and be communicated to the researches for proper moulding of traditional technologies with modern ones. This could certainly help in agricultural production on sustainable basis.

Looking to the present status of women in agriculture and their limited access to research and extension services, it is utmost needed to revamp the entire approach towards women farmers to cater to their existing needs emphasizing the future challenges which the country has to face in the coming years. For this, there is no way but to develop the human resources. Hence, empowerment of women is the need of the day, as it is only the surest way of making women as "partner's in development" and bringing them in the mainstream of development, not only as mere. "Beneficiaries" but also "Contributors". If women are empowered the day is not far away when "Feminization of Agriculture" will be in the offing and the theme "Women Feed the World" will be true in its actual sense.

Strategies are the designed and directed actions following a stipulated pathway to accomplish goals. So on the assessed and identified problems following strategic intervention can be suggested.

Short term strategies:

Emphasis in this phase is to fulfill their basic needs through welfare programmes like :

- Literacy programme
- Family planning programme and health education
- Nutrition programme -for mothers and children
- Portable water and appropriate fuel for cooking and heating the house
- Access to household. technology
- Home economic programme

Mid term strategies:

Emphasis is on facilitating their involvement in economic activities and strengthening their economic base for entering in social and political mainstream of the society. Some strategies at this phase are :

- Access to appropriate technology and financial resources
- Ownership of productive assets
- Attaining income Security through income generating projects
- Access to communication mcdia to improve their communication and mediatior, skills

- Access to and prospering of all types of non-formal education like extension and vocational education in order to improve their entrepreneurial skills.

Long term strategies:

Social and political mainstream are important components of empowerment at high level. Some strategies which can. be applied at this phase are

- Enhancing organizational and social leadership skill in community action
- Building their capacity through collectivization and social political participation.
- Increasing their negotiation power in action for entailment rights.
- Increasing their access to political power, policy formulation and strategic gender training programme
- Establishing organisation or self help groups for their own networking and empowerment through group-building.
- Providing distance education and correspondence courses
- Encouraging socio-cultural changes by exploring gender issues.

Literacy:

Literacy programme is very important in the process of women's empowerment. It is a base for any educational programme. It enables rural women to acquire new knowledge and technology required for improving and developing their tasks in all fields. Literacy helps rural women to bring up their children and carry out the responsibility of motherhood.

Family Planning and Welfare Programme:

Family planning programme and health education are two very important basic needs for empowerment of rural women.

In most of the developing countries, rural women suffer from the strain and burden of frequent pregnancies, lack of access to new methods and suitable contraceptives. This is one factor which affect their lives by with drawing them from participating in the process of development.

Non-Formal Education

Non-Formal Education (NFE) is an effective method of women's empowerment in rural areas. Due to some constrains like lack of sufficient time and higher level of age, it is very difficult to provide formal education to rural women. Therefore, non-formal education is the best vehicle in transferring new knowledge and technology to them NFE for empowerment means people gaining an understanding of and control over social, economic and/ or political forces to improve their standing in society. Some indication of the effect of NFE for empowerment are:

- Increase access to resources
- Increase collective bargaining power
- Improved status, self-esteem and cultured identity.
- Ability to reflect critically and solve problems
- Ability to make choices.
- Legitimisation of people's demands by officials
- Self-discipline and ability to work with others.

Extension Programme:

Rural Women would benefit immensely from modern scientific knowledge, technology and skills. Till recent times, agricultural policies and programmes in most developing countries have generally ignored women's need and concerns as farmers. Only over the last decade, there has been increasing awareness of the extent and significance of women's activities in agriculture. Most developing countries have now started training rural women in new technologies. In spite of recent consideration on launching extension programmes for rural women, some impediments hinder them from reaching extension facilities like.

- Illiteracy
- Financial barriers of govt. and families to invest on women's education.
- Lack of time due to heavy households responsibilities
- Lack of valid statistics and data about the roles needs and problems of rural women.
- Giving less attention to women's enterprises by extension and research centres.
- Less number of educated women to take the responsibilities of extension activities (Female, extension workers).
- Social and cultural barriers in some societies in which contact between women with male extension workers, is prohibited.

There are some appropriate and effective extension educational methods for rural women like.

- Mobile courses instead of farmer's training centre.
- Utilisation of educated girls and widows as female extension workers
- Education of women through negotiation between husband and wife or inter spouse communication.
- Tours and visits organized by women's group or Organization (co-operatives etc.).
- Set up extension organisation for rural women like Pakistan, Sri Lanka and Bangladesh
- Encourage make extension agents to work with group.
- Post female extensionists in their local areas or close to their husband's workplace.
- Working women extensionists in pairs (husband and wife as extensior workers).
- Encourage and support the establishment of local groups and organisations to take up responsibility of communicating new science and technology to rural women.

Community Education

Community education is an integral part of community development and community empowerment is a, way by which people involve in-group efforts to identify their problems, analyse their cultural and socio-economic roots of problems, and develop strategics 'bringing positive change e in their lives and in their communities. It is an ongoing process that demands time and continued commitment towards better quality life and justice for community education can uphold there effective involvement of rural women in building community through collective action. This type of education gives them the power to participate in all aspects of community development and be active citizens. This education will also tackle social and cultural barriers which restrict the participation of rural women in social activities.

Adult Education:

Adult education is another type of non-formal education which is an effective strategies intervention for empowerment of women. This will lead the community to have same impression about the necessity of women's empowerment and pay attention to their gender specific needs. Older people have a lifetime experience, knowledge and wisdom to offer to others in their community. In view point, girl's education in some countries where there are social and cultural barriers for educating females, community level work may help parents understand the value of educating girls. Adults' education classes provide one such opportunity for influencing the thinking of parents.

Access to communication Media:

Access to communication media prepares women for improving their communication and mediation skills to strengthen their capacity to contact and mediate with external world. Consequently, the employment of this skill will prepare the way for transaction of their own experiences, knowledge and work skills with other persons and increase their awareness about the women's rights, allocated facilities, and resources by government or other organisations.

Access to appropriate Technology

Experience show that the technology can be appropriate for rural women when it has the following characteristics:

- Based on their needs and problems
- Cheap, simple and small scale,
- Harmonise and compatible with local materials, resources and cultures
- Locally available skills and knowledge
- Labour and time saving
- Access and control of rural women.

Due to some implements like, lack of access to land, credit, education, lack of recognition and their contributions to village life, rural women don't have suitable access to and control over new technology.

Access to credit:

One factor hindering rural women's empowerment is their limited access to credit and saving schemes. This problem restricts their access to technology, income generating projects, land possession and allotment of resources required for development. In order to have access to credit setting up self help group local banking system by women, non governmental organisation and provision of facilities by govt. need to be established. SEWA as a women's banking founded by Mrs. Ela Bhat in Ahmedabad and indira Mahila Jojna are two successful examples in this direction.

Participation:

Women can be integrated into development process in two ways. Firstly as participants and secondly as beneficiaries of development. Women can be beneficiaries of development, if they are active participants in the development process. They also benefit through greater access to education, employment, improved social services such as health, housing, sanitation and improved technology. Within the development projects, instrumental participation is viewed as a way of achieving certain specific targets; and transformations participation is viewed as an objective itself, and as a means of achieving some higher objective such as self help and or sustainability. Since the goal of empowerment is to meet strategic gender needs proving opportunity for rural women to participate in development programme is not only a way to help community and family but also an occasion for their empowerment.

Work and Empowerment:

- Farming in a small piece of land
- Raising livestock
- Collection of forest produce
- Manufacturing at home or in sheds
- Hawking, vending, trading
- Providing services
- Selling manual labour

One of the important means of achieving empowerment. in the status of women is to promote additional avenues for employment.

Ownership and Control over Resources:

They need to have control over limited resources, like land and livestock, so that they could take away decisions and implement them in any way that is required ownership and control over productive assets Will create a sense of belonging and owning. It will thus help to take responsibility in family and local group activities. Other impact of control is to enhance their decision making ability to meet same physiological needs like self esteem and confidence.

Access to co-operatives and local women's organisation:

Collectivisation has been recognized as a tenant of women's empowerment, It has been defined as a process of bringing a group of women together at a base to become an integral part of an economic. activity. Some impact of collectivization on rural women are :

- Bring about new identities inside the group
- Facilitating their responsibilities through sharing -their information knowledge, experience-skills, time frames, spaces and other resources like money etc.

Some suggestions on empowerment of rural women:

- Increasing their access to new information, credit labour, markets and growing sector of economy.
- Furthering their social and political participation at all levels and overcoming structural barriers to women's full productivity.
- Increasing govt. assistance for the family unit (child care, health care, F.P.P.)
- Facilitating the establishment of organizational structures like farmer's group and organizing them gender sensitivity at all level of planning and implementation of development programmes.
- Increase the economic self-sufficiency of women through self-employment.
- Increase their power of negotiation about redistribution of power resources within households, civil society and the state.
- Strengthening educational and training programmes for them.
- Increasing their access to and over appropriate technology that affect on reducing work burden.

Conclusion

Gender sensitivity and systematic approach are two factors important for rural development programme targeted either at women or both women and men. Empowerment is a complicated process, which comprises of short-term and long-term strategy. Under each strategy, several projects need to be formulated and carried out. The process of women's empowerment is conceptualized in terms of personal assertions and confidence, ability to project themselves as women, attaining economic independence, ownership of productive assets, ability to handle capital and assets and provide leadership in both women and community related issues at all levels.

References

Adick (1995) : Basic Education for Women and girls in rural areas; Agriculture and Rural Development. 2 : 1.

Awasthi, O. N. (1993) : Education Development in India, Journal of Education and Social Change 7 : 1.

Gopalan, S. (1992). Monitoring and Evaluation of the training programmes for women, function areas in rural Development. 11 : 5.

Hernader (1993) : Cultural contributions as a complement to economic incentives for people involve in sustainable development project un rural areas; Landscape and Urban Planning, 27.

Hirawy, J. Vnni (1990); Employment and occupational diversification of women in India.

Horowite et al. (1995) : Gender issues in natural resources management; social aspects of sustainable dryland management.

Raju, B. Y., A. A. Firdansi (1997). Women's development issues, concerns and approaches; Journal of Rural Development, Hyderabad.

Sinha, N. Shi (1991) : Towards the target of full employment, Yojana, 39.

5

Historical Profile of Women in India

Indian society presents a very complex picture of women's status. There are rhetorical and historical evidences of highly empowered womanhood with simultaneous pejorative historical evidences of commodified womanhood. Indian society worships the woman, as the goddess of power (Durga), wealth (Lakshmi), and learning (Sarasvati). At the same time, institutionalization of prostitution from historical times of "devdasi" poses a threat to the woman image of goddess (devi). Paradoxically nevertheless, both the practices of deification and indignation of women image have come to co- exist with normal religious prescriptions in the favour of the devdasi the symbol of powerlessness.

The archaic prevalence of "mother right" as propounded by Bechofen, Bankroft and Morgan depicts an empowered womanhood. Devi worship and Shakti cult in India depict this "mother right" and empowered womanhood. Archaeological evidences in the works of Sir John Marshal reveals that before the Aryan invasions, the local population revered the goddess. Merlin Stone also found that in pre-historic and early historic periods, such religion existed in which people revered their supreme creator as female. Most of the Indian deities are female. The pre-aryan dravidian civilization in Mohan-jo-Daro and Harappa reflected an exalted image of women, prominently represented by mother goddess (Sharma, Tripat 1987).

The Early Vedic Period

The Rig-Veda and the Upanishada bear the testimony of esteemed and exalted womanhood. There seemed to be no gender division in hunting, warfare, defense and political activities. During the Rig Vedic time, family was the unit of political structure, where the woman would rule over the household. At moments of crisis, woman would also join politics and warfare. The Aryans in the early Vedic period were essentially preoccupied with military and semi-military operations, and they were greatly dependent upon womenfolk. (Mukharji Parnjati, 1978).

The overall concern and respect of the society towards women, and their considerable freedom in the different activities in social and political life is appreciable. The girls were educated like boys and had to pass through a period of Brahmacharya. Many of them became distinguishud poets. The age at marriage was not very low, usually done only when the girls achieved full womanhood. Large percentage of girls were fairly conversant with religious rituals. In social and religious functions, they occupied a prominent position. The widow would remarry or follow the custom of "niyoga" and have conjugal relations with her husband's younger brother till she had some children. They could' perform sacrifices independent of men. Another important aspect of empowered woman hood was the practice of "swayamvar" (self choosing of groom)..

Women in the vedic period could also be initiated in vedic studies and were entitled to offer sacrifices to Gods, the son was not absolutely necessary for the purpose. Since girls were married around the age of 16 or 17, the period before marriage was utilized for imparting education to them. They would learn by heart the vedic hymns. Women poets themselves were reported to have been composing hymns.

Some of them were mentioned in the RigVeda. Lopa Mudra, Vishwa Varna, Sikata, Nivavari and Ghosha and contributed to the Vedic hymns. We also come across the names of women scholars such as Sulabha. Maitreyi, Vadava Prathitey, Gargi and Vachaknavi, who had made significant contribution to the advancement of education (Thapar Romila, 1985) .

The Later Vedic Period

The process of deterioration of the status of women started in the later Vedic period, when agricultural civilization started creating surplus and conditions of private property. This was a period of the Atharva Veda. In India, patriarchy started with the advent of the vedic aryan, and particularly with the advent of the sutra period (600-300 B.C.), which marked a departure from strict observance of the early vedas. The hitherto existing political role of the woman was drastically reduced. The later Vedic period was characterized by confinement of common woman to the household. In the Ramayana and the Mahabharata however, the para-political role of the royal class women in state affairs is notable. Kaikey's role in enthroning Bharata by impelling Rama to exile leading to the gross suppression of the prevailing custom of primogeniture in the Ramayana, and the roles of Gandhari, Kunti, and Draupadi in deciding the course of warfare in Mahabharata are important. But, so far as the rank and file was concerned, no evidence is available to generalize any notion of mass political empowerment of women.

On the other hand, inspite of the negation of property rights in the Mahabharata we find the practice of Swayamvara by Draupadi, a practice which is phenomenal so far as decision Making and social empowerment of women is concerned. In more civilized stage such practice is confined to the royal families and could not become common man's practice. The Aryan impact reduced or left no scope of this. However one may find similar practice of self choosing of husband among the tribal communities in India today. But the paradox is, the same Draupadi was a bride of the pandava fraternal polyandry and had to face the eternal humiliation of being stripped when Yudhisthir, the Pandava prima, lost in gambling to the Kauravas, In the Ramayana also a strong evidence of caste division and disadvantaged womanhood symbolised through Shabari) is found. What is more significant in addition is that even Sita had to undergo "fire trial" to prove her chastity after her recovery from the custody of the Ravana. This has a strong reşemblance with the custom of water trial in the Thadou - kuki society in Manipur, with only difference that the male counterpart is also to face this trial jointly with the female. However in most cases the woman counterpart loose the trial.

In Buddhism and Jainism we find a slight elevation of the status of women. The former did away with the stigma attached to the childless widow, denied the gap between male and female children, liberated marriage law, recognised property & educational rights, and the spiritual search for Nirvana for women as well, and institutionalized the courtesans. A greater freedom of the women as Bhikhuni was also recognised. (Chakravarti Uma 1995).

But while the religious status of women was exalted, the difference of status between the nun and the monk is conspicuous. Inside the sanghe, women experienced severe discrimination. Denial of political participation and the practice of polygamy further eroded the social status of women. The roles and images of wife and mother were however common to those prescribed in the brahminical texts.

Jainism granted secondary position to women in the spiritual order as they were considered less physically fit than men in undertaking "self mortification and self effacement", though daughters and the widows enjoyed a slightly better position in the society.

The Caste Phenomenon

In order to get a fuller comprehension of the position of women is? ancient society a brief reference to varna and caste system is relevant. The caste system with the passage of time became stereotyped and rigid and the criteria of birth and sex started to determine the function and social status of the individual. The shift was from achievement to ascription. The social stratification process created a clear hierarchy. It created a caste and gender based division of labor. In agriculture for instance, women could engage in water regulation, transplanting and weeding but not in polishing. The physical mobility of woman was also restricted through caste norms. The territorial division (mohalla) of the villages in India is in fact nothing but caste stereotypes where the mobility of lower caste woman (and also men) is highly restricted. The marriage of a lower caste woman to the upper caste man would create much social commotion while reverse practice would be highly scandalous and would not be approved by the society. The concept of untouchability and impurity was deep rooted in the caste system, and it first abused the shudras (bhangis, chamars etc.) and further the women by identifying them with shudras. The prohibition of the sacred thread ceremony to both women and shudras, similar punishment for killing a shudra or a women, denial of religious privileges to the women etc. are some of the practices indicating the women class. (Altekar, A.S,1962).

In the patrilineal society where considerable concern for ritual purity is emphasized, women play a vital role in the protection of the purity of the groups. Veena Das (1976) remarks "women were literally seen as a point of entrance, as gateway to the caste system. If men of low status were to get sexual access to women of higher status then the main threat to the purity of the group came from female sexuality. It therefore became vital to guard against such ritual. This problem was solved by the custom of pre-puberty marriage".

The Manu code laid down the basic framework for a hierarchical caste structure. patriarchal joint family with the oldest male as the supreme head of the patrilineal kin group, and the subordinate status for the shudras and women. Even the Bhagwat Gita places women, vaishyas and shudras in the same category. "According to Parasar Smriti punishment for killing either a woman or a shudra is identical"(Thapar, Romila, 1985).

The historical roots of such social practices may be found in the process of transition of "mother right" to "father right" that corresponded to the history of economic transition from common property economy to private property economy. Jayswal found that "the growth of a class society - which manifested itself in the form of verns and the decline in the position of women have occurred simultaneously. This decline dates back from the period of Manusmriti 500 BC to 1800 AD." (Jayswal, Suvira, 1981).

R.S. Sharma (1980) contends that "society in the Rigvedic period was still predominantly pastoral & nomadic. It did not produce enough surplus to allow any section of society to be completely subordinated or withdrawn from the process of production". The birth of a daughter became a source of disaster during the later Vedic phase. Education of women which was an accepted norm during the (early) Vedic period slowly began to be neglected and later on the girls were totally denied any access to education. Upanayana or the sacred thread ceremony which was performed to initiate a person into the Vedic studies, was denied to women and shudras by the Manu codes , thus Dosing the doors of any formal education to women. By the 8th century AD the marriageable age for girls was lowered to 9 to 10 years. This gave a final blow to any effort at educating women and the sinister practice of prepuberty marriages began. Girls in the ruling class families did receive some training in military, administration and fine arts. Mainstream life of the upper caste women was confined to the four walls and restricted to serving kin members alone.

The other secondary cause lay in religion. Religion as a superstructure of economy also exerted its influence, though secondarily, to determine the same status of women. Jayswal (1981) wrote that unmarried men and women had no admission to heaven. Gods do not accept any offering from the unmarried. Wife was an absolute necessity in the religious services.

Husbands and wife had to perform the religious rights together. If there was a Yajna the wife had to participate in it. All the tirthas (pilgrimages) had to be accompanied by the wife; otherwise it was believed that one does not get the fruits of pilgrimage. A Vedic Passage goes : "man is only one half' and he is not complete till he is united with a wife. (Jayswal,Suvira, 1981)

Difference in resource control resulting from the origin of private property initiated the process of women disempowerment and initiated the historical threshold of disadvantaged womanhood . The concept of a monogamous family was institutionalized along with the emergence of private property and resource control by the male. In this the women at large were placed in a lord-subordinate relation and basically had one most ordained duty, that of begetting children . The physiological function of reproduction was turned into a social phenomenon and was instrumental to perpetuate the law of inheritance.

Absolute control for male demanded a system of inheritance of property in favour of male children alone to the exclusion of female children, This was incorporated in the cultural system and the concept emerged "Putrarthe kreatebharya". (wife is for begetting male child). In the Atharva Veda we find a drastic change in hitherto existing positive attitude towards women. Son henceforth came to be looked upon as a property, bequeathed to ensure the welfare of the diseased patriarch in the next world. The Atharva Veda also prescribed charms and rituals to ensure the birth of a son as preferred preference to that of a daughter. The latter's birth however was not a source of consternation to the family in Vedic and Upanishads age.

The Indian society like many other traditional societies did mature into a strong patriarchal society in which patriarchal values came to regulate sexuality, reproduction and social production. Patriarchy developed many norms prohibiting and denying women many rights and specific activities. But more suitable expression of patriarchy was made through symbolizing the inferiority of women, highlighting the self-sacrificing pure image of women and prescribing the ritual practices, which over emphasized the dominant role of a woman as a faithful wife and devoted mother. The role of patriarchy started to be institutionalized with the advent of the Aryans, particularly during the sutra period that marked a departure from strict observance of veda. (Pandey, Rekha, 1996)

Manusmriti tended to lower the status of women in various ways. The basic rules for women's behaviour as expressed in the laws of manu insist that a woman must constantly worship her husband as God, even though he is destitute of virtue or a womanizer. Woman should be kept in dependency by her husband because by nature they are passionate and disloyal. The ideal women are those who do not strive to break these bonds of control. The salvation and happiness of women revolve around their virtue and chastity as daughters, wives and widows (Bishler). This theme has again been reiterated by the essence for the creation of the offspring; The role of the mother is just to receive the seed and through her own blood provide warmth and nourishment and help it grow. (Dube, Leela 1978). Dube also says that "one of the most significant aspects of the symbolism is how the two partners are situated in the process of reproduction. In body man and woman are at par with one another in so far as the process of reproduction is concerned. The offspring belongs to the one to whom the seed belongs. In fact he also owns the fields. . (Dube, Leela, 1978).

The implication of the symbolism is that the man is the lord, master, owner or provider. A daughter or a wife is a commodity or a possession. There are rituals and practices for the women which reinforce her role as a devoted wife and doting mother. "Women perform a large number of the yearly calenderical rites, seeking the protection and well being of crucial kinsman (especially husband, brother and son), the general prosperity and health of the family member, with the false consciousness that "by serving their husband only can they win heaven." (Kakkar.S. 1981)

While therefore the origin of family was coterminous with that of private property, the further cultural process was built around biological necessities by beautifying women and adding aesthetic properties to her body.

In Hindu mythology woman has been created by taking the lightness of the leaf and the glance of the mist, the inconsistency of the wind and the timidity of the hare, the vanity of the peacock etc.. The creator added the harshness of the diamond, the sweet flavor of honey, the cruelty of the tiger, the warmth of the fire and the turtledove, and the chill of snow. He melted all these and formed a woman.

The sense of beautification is inherent in the hedonistic principle underlying privatization and subjugation of womanhood. In fact monogamy is the other name of privatized sex which meant an extreme sense of private possession. As monogamy emerged as a matter of convenience to perpetuate inheritance of property in the male line, a "culture of silence" had to be nurtured among the women. The mythology further goes:

"then, he made a present of her to man". The Indian woman's tale is an endless account of woe. They are abandoned, divorced, bought and sold and killed at the mere will of men.

The Later Phase

During the Gupta period one can find concrete civil laws to deal with marriage, ,dowry, inheritance and widow remarriage (information services of India-women in India) within the broad cultural frame of classical patriarchy. The political role of the "mother queen" and "joint rules" in shaping the political history of the imperial Guptas is however significant (Sharma R.S, 1980). But this role was confined only within the royal families and the rank and file was to share the main stream fate with no opportunity of political empowerment. In the social sphere the self choosing of groom (swayamvara) was confined to the royal brides.

Despite the overall social & cultural sub-ordination of women, it is surprising to find that law givers recognized 'the right to property particularly that which was known as streedhan meaning women's property. But this was more of the nature of presentation than right as such. Manu defines streedhan as that which was given to her before the nuptial fire, bridal procession, in token of love and which she has received from brother, mother, father or husband." Later, the law givers, particularly from 7th century had liberally interpreted the term Streedhan by including even property as acquired through inheritance, purchase, partition, chance and adverse possession. This liberal tradition however was subject to various parallel social practices which were equally sanctioned. In Bengal upto the recent past there was a practice called "Salar Dhan". One handful of rice per unit of sale of paddy was set aside and was meant for the unmarried daughters in the family. The accumulated quantity of paddy would be hardly equivalent to the price of a Saree.

Thus in practice women acquisition by inheritance and partition was never an encouraged phenomenon. There was tremendous circumscription to inheritance and acquisition by a widow. Even by encouraging the marriage of the widow to the next brother her scope of inheritance would be scotched.

Another liberal current which to some extent widened the horizon for women was the Bhakti movement. The saints emphasized through devotion to a deity that no intermediary such as a pundit or a purohit was required. The bhaktas vehemently attacked ritualism and over lordship of the brahmans, used the vernacular as a language of communication, and opened the gates of religion for women (Pandey, Rekha, 1996)

Not suprisingly it is the Bhakti movement which produced women saints like Meerabai , Sukubai, Muktabai and Vishnupriya and Lalla in the north, and Aridal, Akka Mahadevi in the south and Bhanabai in the west. But this cult was followed not for the salvation of the collectivity but of the individuals. It could not fundamentally affect deep rooted gender discrimination. The introspective approach in renouncing mundane pursuits hardly left any impact on the society. The cravings for individual renunciation was so deep rooted in this cult that those who followed it, renounced both productive and reproductive role in the society. This movement that is why raises the question of social relevance. Another movement though of slightly different nature was the ascetic movement initiated by Lala Lekhraj Kripalani in 1937 in Sindh. The Brahma Kumari sect in the Sindh society was the product of this movement. Ascetic traditions of Jainism and celibacy were the central concepts in this sect. But this was meant essentially for 'purity' of the body than for social and political empowerment of the 'kumaris'. (Chaudhary, 1996)

But both the Bhakti cult and later, the ascetic cult led by lekhraj had strong patriarchal undertones. In Bhakti cult we find a shift from "devi cult' to "dev cult' whereby god is a male (Girdhar) and "prabhu" (overload). Hence, naturally superior. Emancipation lies in worshipping him. The Brahmakumari sect was an attempt to regulate female sexuality and stimulate self restraint under the claims of reforming the society (Chaudhary, 1996).

Position of Woman During Pre-independence Period

The British rule had followed a double standard so far as the society and economy of India were concerned. The need for cheap labor and exploitation of the natural resources were at the core of the imperial economy and it did not initially touch upon the social system as such and the pre-colonial social structure was dominating the social scene. The liberal imperial economy had converged with the traditional caste ridden India society. Given the choice between the economic interest and social reforms the colonials definitely preferred the former.

The women always were a source of cheap labor force to the British. It is interesting to note that in the coal industry in Bengal the women and child labor was the cheap labor, despite there being a legal ban on it since 1901. In the first two decades of this century female and child labor was in demand for carrying coal underground, since no substitute male labor was available as cheaply." The ban became operational only in 1928 when cheap male labor started to be available. Even then the state recommended that their removal from underground work should be phased out over a period of 10 years. In 1928 29 percent of the underground coal mines workers were female (Sangari Kumkum and Sudesh Vaid , 1989). In such a colonial situation the few social legislations like abolition of Sati act in 1827, the Widow Remarriage act, 1856, Civil Marriage act 1872 seem to be an anachronism.

By the 19th century of social movement, India was facing a twin crisescolonial crisis and social crisis. One was let loose by British imperialism and the other was an indigenous phenomenon. But women questions arose more in the context of the newly emergent educated class to be fitted in with colonial system. The rank. and file could not cope with liberal ideas of the colonials. (in Calcutta in those days the Dutta Sisters (Aur Dutta and Taru Dutta) were the first educated women conversant with English language). Education was largely confined to the middle class males and the women had no immediate gain out of that except perhaps that the poorer section could be used as cheap labor source. The social scene was dominated by usual child marriage, illiteracy, bride burning, ill health, widowhood, confinement and many other related vices. These were accepted as fait accompli by the women.

This was the context of the so called renaissance movement. But this movement did not traverse through a linear path.

One stream was emancipation of the women through restoration of the past. This was essentially revivalist and restorationist. Revival of Vedic feminism was at the core of the movement (Mies, M 1988). Dayananda Saraswati and Swami Vivekananda believed in revival of the old Vedic society presuming to be the ideal society for women.

The other stream was traceabls within traditional Hinduism. Ram Mohan Roy and Ishwarchanda Vidyasagar and De'Rogio were the chief proponents of the movement.

The kulin hypergamy by the upper caste Brahmins in Bengal was one of the most sensational social practice those days. A girl of nine years could be well married off to an outgoing octogenarian in death bed. A movement against this was led by Raja Rammohan Roy of Brahmo Samaj. The British, though had enacted the abolition of Sati act, were always reluctant to execute the act fearing social commotion that was undesirable from social and administrative point of view.

Kulin hypergamy provided context to another social reform movement of the Young Bengal led by De Rogio. (his followers were commonly known as De Rogians).

Both these social movements were at the same wave length, and the impact of European liberalism was strong in both these social movements. Both these movements registered protest against the traditional caste ridden

Hinduism and the evil practices associated with this. But while the De Rogians were totally influenced by the liberal tradition of Europe, Brahmo Samaj did not discard Hinduism as such. It intended to blend western liberal view with Hinduism with greater acceptance of the latter as against the traditional (sanatani) Hindusim. The Brahmo Samaj as such carne to stand as an antithesis to sanatani Hindu religion.

Widowhood was another issue that moved another social reform by Vidyasagar. The social sanction on widow marriage (that was not a banned practice as such) added a stigmatic life to the widows who had to accept celibacy with strict food and nutrition deficient practices, not to speak of lack of education and employment.

A very powerful social movement which helped change the position and attitude towards women was the nationalist particularly during the Gandhian phase. Gandhi had a strong conviction in the inner power of women. Though his own concept of womanhood was a blend of spirituality and rationality, he was an active mobilizer of the women for the cause of the swaraj. He had implanted the concept of Brahmacharya with power for national liberation (Parekh, Bhikhu 1989). He said, "I would love to see that my future army contains a vast preponderance of women over men" In the satyagraha movement men and women took part alike. The evil practices of child marriage, widowhood, polygamy, dowry, temple prostitution, female illiteracy appalled him most. Gandhi conceived that these could be eradicated through the attainment of swaraj. He also believed that it could be obtained only when people are organized. Many women organizations jell in with mahatma's idea. Indian national social council-1887; the women's Indian Association led by Presidency women's Conical-1918; national council of women in India; all India women's conference 1926; are some of the women organizations which came within the fold of Gandhiji. Dr. Annie Besant, theosophist and the first woman president of INC gave a clarion call for the equal status for women. The women salt satyagrahis led by Sarojini Naidu and women in the quit India movement are the examples of an enlightened phase of participation of women for the cause of emancipation of the country in general and of the women in particular. In the militant phase of the freedom movement, Indian women were slowly entering the political field.

For Gandhiji achievement of swaraj was only the first step. He believed that a true swaraj is possible when the disadvantaged people are empowered. There was however conflicting views within the nationalist leaders about the primacy of the social issues to political issues. Gandhiji resolved this conflict by merging political, economic, social issues together in the movement. He never subscribed to the idea that the congress remain as a political party after the attainment of swaraj. He wanted to keep up the profile of the congress as a social organization

A brief reappraisal of the position of the women in the pre independence period reveal two facts (i) a thoroughly passive attitude of the common women (ii) an absence of any significant collective struggle by women (Sangari, K & Vaid,1989). This legacy has come to stay in post independence Indian woman. The independence period started with a general developmental approach to eliminate poverty because of the presence of a number of disadvantaged groups in the country including women. It was only after nearly three decades that the women's issues were brought center stage in 1975. The question of social development posed a bigger question mark on women's development and its centrality vis a vis economic development. It came to be felt that development in the economic and political field have hardly any meaning unless it can address the real problems confronting Indian women in general.

A brief introspection into the history of woman empowerment in India reveals a few important facts

I. Exploitation of woman has a long history
II. It has strong economic motivations
III. Male domination created a cultural superstructure to wrest control property and,'
IV. Use of religion in creating the 'culture of male dominance'
V. Perpetuation of the 'culture of male dominance' and the 'culture of female silence" through glorification of the mother.
VI. Denial of social opportunities and social support to the women
VII. Institutionalizing polygamy and
VIII. Relative docility of women.

Now that the issue of woman empowerment has become a major issue specially after the independence of the country, a large number of literature has generated on the subject.

The impact of global solidarity of women has also exerted tremendous influence on the national literature on women empowerment. Moreover the indigenous perceptions about woman empowerment as found in the classical and neo classical literature are diverse. Hence a linear approach to the issue of women empowerment in India is yet to crystallize.

6

Indicators of Women's Empowerment in India

Women's empowennent, or autonomy, is a multifaceted concept. In a patriarchical society, as exists in large parts of India, men are placed in a more advantageous position than women. The family lineage and living arrangements are centred on man, and inheritance and succession practices tend to neglect women as well. The state of male supremacy is reflected in the child rearing and caring practices. The celebrations for the birth of a male child, and the differential treatment meted out to boys bears ample evidence of this. Access to nutrition, child care and education all favour boys over girls. From a very early age, a girl is socialized to give priority to the needs of the male members in the family. The cumulative effect of these practices is a tilt in the power relations in favour of males. Women's empowerment is essentially an effort to rectify this imbalance and attain gender equity.

Based on a few macrolevel indicators like expectation of life at birth, education and income, the UNDP (2000) has developed a gender-related development index. According to this index, the gender inequity in 1998 is substantially high in India and ranks a poor 108th out of the 143 countries for which the index value is available. In India, a gender gap in literacy still persists, though it has narrowed over the years. For example, at the dawn of independence, according to the 1951 census, only nine per cent of females were literate, compared to 27 per cent of males. Female literacy improved faster than males and after 50 years, the level of literacy for females and males is 54 and 75 per cent; respectively. The differentials are particularly wide in the states of Bihar and Uttar Pradesh.

A similar pattern can be observed in the case of increased life expectancy. Unlike most countries, the longevity of males is higher than that of females in India and has been so for a long time. In recent years, owing to improvements in the female life expectancy, female life expectancy has exceeded male life expectancy marginally. Notwithstanding, female child mortality continues to be much higher compared to males, particularly in the north of the country.

Marriage practices also have an immense influence on women's position in family. In fact, a difference in marriage customs between north and south India has been identified as a factor responsible for the differential level of women's status (Dyson and Moore, 1983). In southern India marriages often occur between relatives. In such consanguineous marriages, brides do not go into a completely unknown family. Marriages in the south are generally endogamous, and brides maintain their link with the natal family. In contrast, marriages in the north are exogamous and a bride goes into a completely unknown family, causing the link with her natal family to weaken.

There are studies which have highlighted the role of gender in understanding demographic diversity within the country. They suggest that women's status is an important variable responsible for the lower level of fertility in the south, compared to the north. Bardhan (1974) suggested that widespread rice cultivation in the south, which is female labour intensive, contributes positively towards the economic value of a woman and is possibly a contributing factor for lower fertility in the south than in the north of India. Dyson and Moore (1983) and later Malhotra, Vanneman and Kishore (1995) further investigated the north-south dichotomy in the demographic transition and emphasized the role of gender equality in this context. It was confirmed that patriarchy and development play a strong role in defining regional variations in fertility levels in India. Aspects of patriarchy are both overlapping and multidimensional in their relationship to fertility: gender discrimination and marriage systems overlap considerably, while women's economic value is relatively independent of the other two dimensions.

Studies on women's empowernent as such, are rare. There is a lack of knowledge regarding different dimensions of women's autonomy and specific strategies to enhance it. Laws and institutional rules can support the endeavour of women's empowerment, but considering the complex cultural beliefs and practices that lie at the root of the imbalance, the effectiveness of such isolated efforts remains doubtful

In the absence of appropriate measures of empowerment, commonly found measures like education and employment are used as surrogates. While those proxy measures are important and are ideally associated with empowerment, they may not capture all aspects of the multidimensional concept of empowerment (Joshi, 1999).

At the family/household level, gender inequity manifests itself in a weaker role for women in decision-making, lesser control ove.- resources and restrictions in physical movement. According to Jejeebhoy (1998) ".... while women's autonomy is indeed multidimensional, at least three dimensions – decision-making, mobility and access to economic resources — are closely related in all settings, irrespective of region or religion".

The recently conducted national family health survey, collected information on a variety of aspects related to the status of women and is a reliable resource to understanding different dimensions of women's autonomy in India. Using the above data, the present paper attempts to examine the following

- Variation in the level of female autonomy in different sociocultural settings such as religion, caste, economic status and family type.
- Role of the indirect (proxy) indicators such as education. work participation, age and educational difference between spouses in understanding women's empowerment.
- Extent to which indirect indicators and direct indicators like decision-making, freedom of movement and access to money help facilitate women in gaining control over the circumstances of their lives (like self-esteem, favourable attitude towards girls' education and family planning practices).

Data and methodology

The NFHS survey undertaken in 1998-1999 covered a representative sample of more than 90,000 eligible women aged 15-49 from 26 states that existed at that time. For the present study, two states were chosen: Uttar Pradesh (including the present Uttaranchal) from the north and Tamil Nadu from the south of India. Uttar Pradesh and Tamil Nadu lie at two extremes of the demographic, social and cultural dimensions of India. The findings revealed that the total fertility rate in Uttar Pradesh was 3.99, which is much higher than 2.19 in Tamil Nadu. Similarly, the mortality rate was much lower in Tamil Nadu than in Uttar Pradesh. For example, the infant mortality rate was 87 per 1,000 live births in Uttar Pradesh compared to 48 in Tamil Nadu. Female literacy was much higher in Tamil Nadu (59 per cent) than in Uttar Pradesh (43 per cent) (IIPS and ORC Macro, 2000). Both states are typically patriarchal and patrilocal and the northern region is well known for inegalitarian gender relations (Jejeebhoy, 1998). In order to understand the suitable indicators of women's empowerment and their influence, this study examines the indicators in two different sociocultural settings. This attempt will also hopefully facilitate an understanding of the north-south divide in women's equality. In Uttar Pradesh, the survey covered a total of 8,682 households and 9,292 eligible women. The analysis in this study is based on 8,012 currently married women who are the usual residents of the households. In Tamil Nadu, the survey covered a sample of 5,281 households, 4,676 eligible women, but the present analysis is only based on 4,028 currently married women who are permanent residents.

The variables related to women's empowerment have been categorized into three groups. The first category is referred to as indirect indicators of empowerment and includes education, occupation, age difference education difference between spouses. These indicate the characteristics that have relevance in influencing a woman's access to and control over resources. The next group is direct indicators of empowerment, and consists of indicators such as involvement in decision-making, freedom of movement and access to money. These indicators tend to provide evidence of empowerment (see Kishor, 1998 for a comprehensive discussion of the indicators). However, empowerment is a multidimensional concept, which purports to measure a woman's ability to control resources, her ability to choose and control different outcomes, and above all enhance her self-esteem. Our third set of indicators relates to a few additional dimensions of empowerment that the survey captures, and was referred to as evidence of empowerment. This category is comprised of three indicators, namely, extent of self-esteem, favourable attitude towards girls' education and practice of family planning.

In the survey, each woman was asked six questions to assess her attitude towards wife beating. The questions relate to whether, according to the respondent, a husband is justified in beating his wife for each of the following reasons: if he suspects her of being unfaithful, if her natal family does not pay the promised dowry, if she shows disrespect towards her in-laws, if she goes out without telling him, if she neglects the house or children; or if she does not cook food properly. A woman's self-esteem is considered high if she does not agree with any of these reasons a, justification for a husband to beat his wife, otherwise her self-esteem is considered low.

A question was asked in the survey to each woman about her attitude towards girls'/boys' education. The specific question about girls' education asked was: "In your opinion, how much education should be given to girls these days". Based on the responses, a variable was computed to determine whether a woman has a favourable attitude towards girls' education. If according to a woman, the extent of education to be given to a girl is greater than or equal to that of a boy, she is regarded as having a favourable attitude, otherwise she is not seen as having a favourable attitude.

In addition to all those indicators of empowerment, the authors have considered five background characteristics of women to understand the variation in the autonomy in different sociocultural settings such as caste, religion, place of residence, standard of living and the type of family structure.

Results

In the following section, the analysis on the relationship between the indirect and direct measures of autonomy is presented. An attempt is also made to examine how those indicators, in turn, are associated with the characteristics which provide evidence of empowerment.

Indirect visa-vis direct measures of autonomy

In the absence of direct data on women's autonomy, previous studies have relied on other measures – years of education,

Table 1. Percentage of usual residents and currently married women involved in decision-making about their own healih care, percentage with freedom of movement and percentage with access to money by indirect indicators of female autonomy

Indirect indicators	Uttar Pradesh				Tamil Nadu			
	Percentage involved in decisions about own health care	Percent -age with complete freedom of move -ment	Percent -age with control over economic resources[s]	Number of women	Percentage involved in decisions about own health care	Percent -age with complete freedom of move -ment	Percent -age with control over economic resource[s]	Number of women
Education								
Illiterate	43.0	9.6	46.2	5,677	58.0	53.8	76.1	1.882
Literate up to Middle	46.0	8.7	58.7	930	60.8	51.2	7,9.2	932
Middle	50.1	15.1	69.1	1,405	57.1	51.4	82.0	1.213
Occupation								
Not working	43.1	9.6	50.3	6,120	56.5	47.7	77.0	1.920
Working not for cash	49.0	122	51.8	1,058	63.8	57.0	78.1	466
Working for cash	49.9	14.4	61.6	833	59.3	55.7	80.4	1.699
Age difference between spouses								
Little (5 years)	43.9	10.2	503	5.117	60.7	53.5	79.4	1,821
Moderate (6-10 years)	45.7	11.2	54.9	2.092	56.5	523	79.2	1,605
Big (>10 years)	45.4	9.7	52.1	72'2	56.2	49.5	743	598
Education difference between spouses								
No difference	45.3	11.4	48.8	2.682	56.8	55.3	79.4	968
Moderate (5 classes)	46.3	10.5	56.7	2.479	59.8	51.7	78.1	2,346
Big (more than 5 years)	42.5	9.6	50.1	2,820	55.9	56.8	78.9	708
Total	44.6	10.5	51.7	8,012	58.4	52.5	78.6	4,028

[s] access to money.

work-force participation, marital age and spousal age difference as proxies for autonomy. Table 1 presents the bivariate associations between the indirect measures or proxies and the direct measures of female autonomy. As expected, all the three indicators of autonomy suggest that, compared to Uttar Pradesh, women in Tamil Nadu have greater autonomy. A higher proportion of women in Tamil Nadu are involved in decision-making about their own health care, have greater freedom of movement and access to money than women in Uttar Pradesh.

Particularly striking is the low level of freedom of movement in Uttar Pradesh. Only 11 percent of the women in the state mentioned that they have complete freedom of movement—meaning they do not need permission to either go to the market or visit their friends or relatives.

The relationship between the indirect and direct measures of autonomy differs in the two states. The two indirect indicators; education and occupation of women show a stronger association with the three direct indicators of autonomy in Uttar Pradesh than in Tamil Nadu. In fact, in Tamil Nadu the associations are found to be insignificant. In Uttar Pradesh, as the level of education of women improves, their autonomy also increases. A much higher proportion of women who have completed at least a middle level of education are involved in decision-making, have freedom of movement and also have access to money, as compare with women who are illiterate. In Tamil Nadu, where the patriarchy is relatively weak compared to Uttar Pradesh, education, the most commonly used proxy indicator of autonomy, fails to show a clear association with the direct measure of autonomy. Contrary to this, Jejeebhoy found that in a setting where patriarchy is strong other traditional factors can counteract and make the empowering effect of education less significant, than in a setting where patriarchy is weak (Jejeebhoy, 1998). However, it is possible that in a setting where the level of female literacy is generally low, the literate women, particularly those who are educated at least up to a middle level are a select group. Other sources of empowerment such as family background, exposure to the outside world etc. are likely to be high and add to the creation of a positive empowering environment.

Work participation also tends to have beneficial effects in improving women's autonomy. A study by Sharma (1983) states that the women's status in the family is related to whether she is engaged in a gainful economic activity or not. Improved women's autonomy is noticeable among those who work outside for cash and is evident among women in Uttar Pradesh. The other two indirect indicators, age and educational difference between spouses, show no definite relationship with the three direct indicators of autonomy.

Table 2 presents the relationship between the sociocultural setting of women and the direct measures of autonomy. In other words, it shows how female autonomy as indicated by involvement in decision-making, freedom of movement and control over resources varies according to characteristics like caste, religion, residence, standard of living and type of family. The proportions shown against each category of the characteristics have been adjusted to take into account the differences in the levels of the indirect indicators (education, occupation, age and educational difference between spouses). The differentials are found to be larger in Uttar Pradesh compared to those in Tamil Nadu.

The most noticeable difference in the level of sociocultural setting of women and the direct measures of autonomy occurs in the type of family characteristic. Interestingly, the presence of in-laws in a family lowers the level of autonomy of women. Women living in joint families with their in-laws have the lowest levels of autonomy. Specifically, in Uttar Pradesh, women staying in nuclear families have the highest level of autonomy in terms of all three indicators. Another factor that is important in this context is the place of

Table 2. Percentage of usual residents and currently married women involved (adjusted) in decision-making about their own health care, percentage with freedom of movement and percentage with access to money by background characteristics

Background characteristics	Uttar Pradesh			Tamil Nadu		
	Percentage involved in decisions about own health care	Percentage with complete freedom of movement	Percentage with control over economic resources	Percentage involved in decisions about own health care	Percentage with complete freedom of movement	Percentage with control over economic resources
Caste						
SC/ST	57.4	25.9	83.4	66.3	62.5	92.8
Others	62.8***	22.1**	85.2**	67.3	62.1	93.0
Religion						
Hindus	61.4	23.0	84.3	67.0	62.7	93.0
Non-Hindus	63.1	22.6	87.2***	67.9	58.1*	92.9
Place of residence						
Urban	65.6	27.9	89.3	70.1	66.1	93.8
Rural	60.6**	21.7**	83.4***	65.4**	60.0***	92.4*
Standard of living						
Low	62.2	22.9	80.3	65.7	61.9	91.5
Medium	62.0	21.9	85.2***	68.5	63.1	93.3***
High	59.8	26.1	89.4***	65.6	60.0	94.4***
Type of family						
Broken/Suppl. extended	62.5**	23.2***	85.7***	65.8	65.0***	92.7***
Nuclear	63.7***	28.0***	87.1***	67.1	63.6***	93.8***
Joint without in-laws	61.9**	24.4***	85.4***	69.3	58.3*	92.9***
Joint with in-laws	57.6	15.5	79.5	66.7	51.7	84.1

$Adjusted for usually used proxy indicators of female autonomy mentioned in table 1.

*** $p<0.001$ ** $p<0.05$ * $p<0.10$

residence. Women living in rural areas are found to have less autonomy than urban women.

Autonomy and evidence of empowerment

It is expected that the different dimensions of autonomy should facilitate and culminate in greater self-esteem and a positive attitude towards the girl child among women. If a woman agrees and admits that a husband is justified in beating his wife for any of the reasons asked in the survey, she is seen as not fully empowered. Table 3 provides information on such associations.

At the outset, it is apparent that a much higher proportion of women in Uttar Pradesh have high self-esteem than women in Tamil Nadu. But, women in Tamil Nadu have a more equitable attitude towards educating girl children and a higher propensity to use family planning methods, as compared to women in Uttar Pradesh. Thirty-eight percent of the women in Uttar Pradesh subscribe to the view that a husband is not justified in beating his wife under any of the circumstances asked in the survey. In Tamil Nadu, the percentage of such women is much lower (26 per cent). By and large, the different direct indicators of autonomy are positively related to the indicators of empowerment. Freedom of movement shows the strongest association with the empowenment indicators. In Tamil Nadu. 31 per cent of women with complete freedom of movement showed greater self-esteem, compared to only 21 percent of women without freedom of movement.

It is surprising to find that women in Tamil Nadu tend to accept wife beating more than those in Uttar Pradesh. It may be mentioned in this context, that a greater proportion of women in Tamil Nadu have reported being beaten than in Uttar Pradesh. It may not be out of context to mention that the survey showed a much higher proportion of males in Tamil Nadu drink alcohol than those in Uttar Pradesh

Table 3. Percentage of permanent, who are currently married and do not agree with justifications given for a husband beating his wife (self-esteem), percentage with no unwanted pregnancy and percentage using family planning (by direct indicators of female autonomy)

Women status	Uttar Pradesh				Tamil Nadu			
	Percent-age with greater self-esteem	Percent-age favour girls' education	Percent-age using family plan-ning	Number of women	Percent-age with greater self-esteem	Percent-age favour girls' education	Percent-age using family plan-ning	Number of women
Decision-making in health care								
Respondent involved	39.1	55.6	33.1	3,528	31.5	57.6	54.2	2.34.3
Not involved	36.9	51.3	27.1	4,370	19.0	56.5	51.9	1.674
Freedom of movement								
Complete freedom	45.7	66.3	40.3	827	31.3	61.3	55.3	2.103
No complete freedom	37.0	51.7	28.5	7,065	20.7	52.6	51.0	1.914
Control over resources								
Yes	37.7	56.4	34.4	4,083	27.6	57.2	53.6	3.146
No	38.1	49.8	24.9	3.778	21.4	56.8	51.7	857
Total	37.9	53.2	29.8	7,897	26.3	57.0	53.3	4.018

(IIPS and ORC Macro, 2001) and alcohol abuse have been found to be a factor leading to domestic violence.

The relationship of the indirect measures of autonomy and the sociocultural settings to the factors of evidence of empowerment was also examined in this study. The three indicators of evidence of empowerment were evaluated separately and the results are shown in tables 4 to 6. Three separate logistic regression models have been used for each of the indicators.

Attitude towards wife beating

Direct indicators of autonomy, particularly whether a woman has complete freedom of movement, shows a significant association with her attitude towards wife beating in both states. For example, in Tamil Nadu. a relatively higher proportion of women with freedom of movement deplore wife beating, compared to those not having freedom of movement (table 4). Autonomy in decision-making also leads to higher self-esteem in Tamil Nadu, but not in Uttar Pradesh. Control over resources does not lead to a favourable disposition of women towards wife beating in Tamil Nadu. One surprising result is that in Uttar Pradesh a lower proportion of women with control over resources show high self-esteem compared to those with no control over resources. In this context, it may be mentioned that the proportion of women working for cash is much higher among those who say they have control over resources than those who claim to have no control over resources. The majority of women working for cash are agricultural labourers or unskilled or skilled manual workers. These women are found to have lower self-esteem, compared to women who are either home makers or working not for cash or are in professional jobs/service sector. The education level of women is found to be an important indicator showing a positive influence on empowerment. However, a moderate level of education does not help in strengthening self-esteem among women. In fact, in Tamil

Table 4. Adjusted proportion of currently married women (usual residents of the household) not agreeing with reasons given in the survey to justify the husband beating his wife (self-esteem) - Results from logistic regression analysis[$]

Background characteristics	Uttar Pradesh			Tamil Nadu		
	Model -I	Model -II	Model -III	Model -I	Model -II	Model -III
Decision-making in health care						
Respondent not involved	41.6	42.5	43.1	30.1	27.0	35.0
Respondent involved	43.3	43.3	43.8	43.3***	40.0***	49.4***
Freedom of movement						
No complete freedom	41.4	42.2	42.7	32.6	29.2	37.3
Complete freedom	50.2***	48.5***	49.7***	42.4***	39.2***	48.8***
Control over economic resources						
No	42.9	45.7	46.2	35.1	32.8	41.6
Yes	41.8	40.3***	40.9***	38.3	34.7	43.7
Education						
Illiterate		38.4	39.9		30.9	47.7
Literate up to middle		43.7***	43.1		28.9	36.7**
Middle+		61.0***	58.0***		44.5***	50.9***
Occupation						
Not working		43.9	44.4		35.8	44.4
Working not for cash		38.5***	38.7***		35.7	44.9
Working for cash		41.0	42.4		32.2*	41.6
Place of residence						
Urban		50.2	49.9		38.3	46.1
Rural		41.0	41.8***		32.2***	41.7**
Age difference between spouses						
Little		42.9	43.5		36.1	45.4
Moderate		43.2	43.2		33.5	41.9*
Big		41.4	43.1		31.1*	40.3*
Education difference between spouses						
Little		41.3	42.4		34.3	43.2
Moderate (5 classes)		43.1	43.6		34.1	43.2
Big (more than 5 years)		44.2*	44.2		34.8	43.5
Caste						
SC/ST			43.8			40.9
Others			41.6			44.0
Religion						
Hindus			42.6			42.4
Non-Hindus			43.6			50.0**
Standard of living						
Low			41.5			41.3
Medium			42.2			40.7
High			50.2***			55 8***
Type of family						
Broken/Suppl. extended nuclear			43.6			43.5
Nuclear			41.7*			4.3.7
Joint without in-laws			44.8			42.6
Joint with in-laws			44.9			40.3

[$] controlled for age of the respondent *** p,0.001 ** p,0.05 * p<0.10

Nadu, a significantly lower proportion of women with a moderate level (literate but below middle) of education are found to have self-esteem compared to illiterates women. As a whole, the sociocultural differentials tend to narrow down when the direct and indirect measures of autonomy are significant.

Attitude tcwards girls' education

Besides indirect measures of autonomy, direct indicators such as freedom of movement and control over resources show a significant impact on the existence of a favourable attitude towards girls' education in both the cultures (table 5). in most Indian societies, girls' education is adversely affected because they are required to assist their mothers in daily household chores. The boys on the other hand, are free from such responsibilities and are sent to schools. However, the situation seems to be changing along with the changing attitudes of women and the realization of the importance of education in the modern era. Respondents with some level of education favoured a reduced gap between boys' and girls' education. Women living in urban areas have shown a more favourable attitude towards girls' education compared to women living in rural areas. The idea that girls should receive as much education as boys has not been widely accepted in rural areas, even today.

Contraceptive use

The more education a woman has, the more likely she is to use contraceptive methods. This link between a woman's education level and contraceptive use is found to be strong. Furthermore contaceptive use is greater among women living in urban areas than among women living in rural areas. Among the direct indicators of autonomy, women with greater control over econoinic resources use contraceptives more than women without cantrol over resources. This is particularly evident in Utter Pradesh (table 6). In short, the

Table 5. Adjusted proportion of currently married women (usual residents of the household) who favour girls' education to be equal or more than the boys' education - Results from logistic regression analysis'

Background characteristics	*Uttar Pradesh*			*Tamil Nadu*		
	Model -I	*Model -II*	*Model -III*	*Model -I*	*Model -II*	*Model -III*
Decision-making in health care						
Respondent not involved	62.7	62.1	64.3	60.9	61.9	61.9
Respondent involved	65.1	63.7	66.3*	60.1	60.8	60.9
Freedom of movement						
No complete freedom	62.4	61.6	64.0	55.6	56.2	55.9
Complete freedom	74.1***	72.8***	74.6**'	64.8***	65.7***	66.0***
Control over economic resources						
No	61.1	62.4	65.1	61.7	64.2	64.1
Yes	66.2***	63.2	65.4	60.1	60.4*	60.6*
Education						
Illiterate		57.6	61.4		54.9	55.2
Literate up to middle		65.6***	66.7**		60 4***	61.1***
Middle		78.9***	77.6***		70.9***	70.3***
Occupation						
Not working		63.8	66.0		63.5	63.5
Working not for cash		61.1*	64.2		58.6	59.4
Working for cash		57.3**	60.3***		59.4*	59.2*
Place of residence						
Urban		73.9	74.3		66.9	67.0
Rural		59.7***	62.6***		58.1***	58.1***
Age difference between spouses						
Little		63.0	65.3		61.5	61.6
Moderate		62.2	64.5		62.3	62.2
Big		63.4	66.6		57.8	58.0
Education difference between spouses						
Little		61.1	64.1		60.3	60.2
Moderate (5 classes)		62.6	65.2		61.4	61.6
Big (more than 5 years)		64.7**	66.2		61.9	62.0
Caste						
SC/ST			63.2			63.7
Others			65.8*			60.6
Religion						
Hindus			65.2			612
Nun-Hindus			65.4			62.6
Standard of living						
Low			62.8			61.6
Medium			62.5			59.5
High			75.9***			65.9
Type of family						
Broken'Suppl.extended nuclear			65.1			62.5
Nuclear			63.8**			60.7
Joint without in-laws			65.0			62.3
Joint with in-laws			67.5			61.9

' controlled forage of the respondent *** p-0.001 ** p-0.05 * p-0.10

Table 6. Adjusted proportion of currently married women (usual residents of the household) who are currently using family planning - Results from logistic regression analysis

Background characteristics	*Uttar Pradesh*			*Tamil Nadu*		
	Model -I	*Model -II*	*Model -III*	*Model -I*	*Model -II*	*Model -III*
Decision-making in health care						
Respondent not involved	38.9	66.7	62.3	45.8	75.6	79.8
Respondent involved	43.7***	68.3	64.0	50.8	74.4	78.9
Freedom of movement						
No complete freedom	40.0	67.2	62.7	43.4	74.1	78.6
Complete freedom	50.2***	69.0	65.4	53.6**	75.7	79.8
Control over economic resources						
No	36.0	65.9	61.7	40.7	76.3	81.0
Yes	45.9***	68.8**	64.3**	50.9	74.5	78.7
Education						
Illiterate		62.5	59.5		73.3	77.8
Literate up to middle		72.3	66.6***		77.7**	81.5**
Middle+		81.1	73.9***		75.2	79.7
Occupation						
Not working		66.7	62.4		75.6	80.0
Working not for cash		69.9	64.9		70.2**	74.1**
Working for cash		68.8	65.2		75.3	79.5
Place of residence						
Urban		76.2	72.2		78.0	81.9
Rural		64.9	60.5***		73.1***	77.7***
Age difference between spouses						
Little		66.2	61.8		74.9	79.2
Moderate		70.9	66.5***		76.2*	80.4
Big		65.6	61.3		71.3	76.1*
Education difference between spouses						
Little		63.8	61.0		75.7	80.3
Moderate (5 classes)		65.6	61.7		74.4	78.7
Big (more than 5 years)		72.1	66.2***		75.6	79.7
Caste						
SC/ST			62.8			77.8
Others			63.1			79.7
Religion						
Hindus			65.3			79.7
Non-Hindus			51.4***			75.9*
Standard of living						
Low			56.2			78.1
Medium			63.5***			79,9
High			71.8***			79.8
Type of family						
Broken/Suppl. extended nuclear			60.7			79.3***
Nuclear			65.1*			8().9***
Joint without in-laws			63.2			767***
Joint with in-laws			61.1			69.9

* controlled forage of the respondent *** p<0.001 ** p<0.05 * p<0.10

level of contraceptive use depends on wornen's autanomy, as well as the usual socioreligious characteristics.

Conclusion

There exists a regional divide in the level of women's empowerment. As expected, women in Tamil nadu have greater autonomy in making decisions regarding their own health care, freedom of movement and access to money. However, empowerment being a multidimensional concept, the results show some interesting variations. Women in Uttar Pradesh are found to have greater self-esteem in the sense that they are more critical about wife beating. A much higher proportion of women in Uttar Pradesh deny that a husband is justified in beating his wife under any of the six circumstances on which data was collected., compared to women in Tamil Nadu. Among the indirect measures of autonomy, education in particular is important and plays a positive role in enhancing different dimensions of autonomy. There are sociocultural variations in the level of empowerment. The type of family in which a woman lives has a strong association with the three direct measures of autonomy. Women staying in families with in-laws show a far lower level of autonomy than do women who live in other types of families.

Of the three direct measures of autonomy, like involvement decision-making, freedom of movement and aocess to money, women particularly in Uttar Pradesh, have the least autonomy in terms of freedom of movement, which turns out to be an important indicator of the evidence of empowerment

Further, women with education, particularly secondary education, and working working women show greater serf-esteem, have a favourable attitude towards girls' education and use contraceptives across cultures. Urban women as compared to rural women are more favourable towards girls' education and towards family planning methods. This divide indicates that there are two different societies that exist in India, a rural culture and an urban culture. In rural areas, the lifestyle is oriented more towards the community than towards the family, while in urban areas, life is more individualistic and family-oriented. The degree of such adherence to societal norms and practices in rural areas is much stronger in Uttar Pradesh than in Tamil Nadu. Among the three selected direct indicators of empowerment, complete freedom of movement determines greater self-esteem and a more favourable attitude for girls' education to a great extent in both cultures.

References

Bardhan, Pranab K. (1974). "On life and death questions", *Economic and Political Weekly, No.* 9, pp. 1293-1304.

Dyson, T. and M. Moore (198+). On kinship structure, female autonomy and demographic behavior". *Population and Development Review, vol.* 9, No. 1, pp. 35-60.

International Institute for Population Sciences (IIPS) and ORC Macro (2000). National Familv Health Survey (NFHS-2), 1998-1999: India, Mumbai: UPS.

Jejeebhoy S. (1998). "Women's autonomy in rural India: Its dimensions, determinants and the influence of context", in Harriet B.Presser and Gita Sen, eds., *Women's Empowerment and Demographic Processes* by 1U SSP, Oxford University Press. pp. 204-238.

Joshi S. T. (1999). Women and development- The changing scenario, New Delhi: Mittal Publications. Kishor S. (1998). "Empowerment of women in Egypt and links to the survival and health of their infants", in Harriet B. Presser and Gita Sen, eds., *Women's Empowerment and Demographic Processes* by IUSSP, Oxford University Press, pp. 119-156.

Malhotra, Vanneman and Kishore (1995). "Fertility, dimensions of patriarchy, and development in India", *Population and Development Review, vol.* 21, No. 2, PP. 281-305

Sharma U. (1983). Women's work and property in North-West India, London: Tavistock Publications. UNDP (2000). "Human Development Report 2000", New Delhi: Oxford University Press.

7

Women Empowerment in India - Milestones & Challenges

Empowerment is seen as a process to gain control over material assets, intellectual resources. Empowerment is defined as a process of awareness and conscientization, of capacity building leading to greater participation, effective decision-making power, control leading to transformative action ability get what one wants and to influence others. The power relation that has to be involved includes their lives at multiple levels, family, community, market and the state. Importantly it involves at the psychological level women's ability to assert themselves and this is constructed by the 'gender roles' assigned to her specially in a cultural which resists change like India.

Women empowerment has become critical to the human rights based approaches to development. The Cairo conference in 1994 organized by UN on Population and Development called attention to women's empowerment as a central focus and UNDP developed the Gender Empowerment measure (GEM) which focuses on the three variables that reflect women's participation in society - political power or decision-making, education and health. 1995 UNDP report was devoted to women's empowerment and it declared that if human development is not engendered it is endangered a declaration which almost become a lei motif for further development measuring and policy planning. Equality, sustainability and empowerment were emphasized and the stress was, that women's emancipation does not depend on national income but is an engaged political process.

Drawing from Amartya Sen's work on 'Human capabilities' - an idea drawn from Aristotle a new matrix was created to measure human development. The emphasis was that we need to enhance human well being flourishing and not focus on growth of national income as a goal.

People's choices have to be enlarged and they must have economic opportunities to make use of these capabilities. States and countries would consider developments in terms of whether its people lead a long healthy painless life or no are educated and knowledgeable and enjoy decent standards of living.

The intuitive idea behind the capability is twofold according to Martha Nussbaum (2003) first, that there are certain functions that are particularly central to human life. Second, that there is something do these in a truly human way, not a mere animal way. The list of capabilities that she draws is cross-cultural as necessary element of truly human functioning. They include:

Life-being able to live to the end of human life of normal length: not dying prematurely, or before one's life is so reduced as to be not worth living.

Bodily health-being able to have good health including reproductive health, to be adequately nourished; to have adequate shelter.

Bodily integrity - Being able to move freely from place to place, to be secure against violent assault, including sexual assault and domestic violence; having opportunities for sex satisfaction and for choice in matters of reproduction.

Senses, imagination and thought - Being able to use the sense, to imagine, think and reason in a truly human way including but not limited to literacy. Being able to use one's mind and imagination protected by freedom of expression.

Emotions - being able to have attachments, to love, to grieve to experience longing gratitude and justified anger. Not having one's emotional development blighted by fear and anxiety.

Practical Reason - Being able to form a conception of the good and to engage in, critical reflection about planning of one's life's protected by liberty of conscience.

Affiliation - Being able to live with and toward others to have social interactions, to have the capability of both justice and friendship. This would entail freedom of assembly and free speech. Having social bases for self-respect and non-humiliation, being protected against discrimination on the basis of race, sex sexual orientation religion caste or region.

Other species - Being able to concern with nature.

Play - being able to laugh, play and enjoy.

Control over one's environment.

a) Political. Being able to participate effectively in political choices that govern one's life, having the right to political participation, protection of free speech and association.
b) Material. Being able to hold property to seek employment on equal bases and having freedom from unwarranted search and seizure. In work, being able to work as a human being, exercising practical reason and entering into meaningful relationships of mutual recognition with the workers.

These capabilities cover the so called "first generation rights" (political & civil liberties) as well as the "second generation rights" (economic and social rights). It has been emphasized that women all over the world have been short shifted and have not found support for their central human functions. Women are capable of these functions given sufficient, nutrition, education and other support. Women are most often not treated as subjects. Women are as capable as men of exercising will, controlling desires and taking decisions but males enjoy support of social institutions and women are excluded as the 'other'. Women are often rot treated as "ends in themselves" persons with dignity who deserve respect from laws and institutions instead they are treated instrumentally as reproducers, caregivers; sexual receivers, agents of family's general prosperity.

Human development report since 1999 demonstrate that practically no country in the world treats its women as well as men according to the measures of life expectancy wealth and education. Developing countries present especially urgent problems when caste and class result in acute failure of human capabilities of women. Women in this part of south East Asia lack essential support for fully functioning human lives. Within the country there are many issues to be addressed closely.

GDI: Inter State Comparison

The virtues of a measure such as the GDI; which can project the status of women by encapsulating achievements in three basis dimensions, soon become clear to policy makers. it spurred efforts to rank States in India by calculating their GDI (Shiv Kumar 1966, Seeta Prabhu, Sarkar and Radha 1996; Aasha Kapur Mehta 1996; Hirway and Mahadevia 1996). A comparison of the HDI and GDI reveal that in Punjab, Haryana, Bihar. West Bengal and Rajasthan development has been inequitous and women did not get equal share in the development. For Uttar Pradesh which has the lowest HDI rank as well as the lowest GDI rank, the challenge is to see how men and women can more from being equal partners in slow development tc partners in dynamic growth.

Empowerment of women is a commitment for PACS and some others strategic programmes, while developing strategies for empowering women some programmes are sensitive to recognizing women's contribution and their knowledge as the first step. The appreciate that women require principally social support to fight their sense of inadequacy and fears to enhance their self-respect and dignity. Empowering women means control over their bodies and becoming economically independent, controlling resources like land and property and reduction of burden of work. A society or programme which aims at women's empowerment needs to create and strengthen sisterhood and to promote overall nurturing, caring and gentleness. PACS emphasis on emphasis on women SHG's as a collective is one such efforts. Being conference 1995 had identified certain quantitative and qualitative indicators of women empowerment.

Beijing conference 1995 indicators of women empowerment, qualitative & quantitative Qualitative:

1. increase in self-esteem, individual and collective confidence;
2. increase in articulation, knowledge and awareness on health, nutrition reproductive rights, law and literacy;
3. increase an decrease in personal leisure time and time for child care;
4. increase on decrease of work loads in new programmes;
5. change in roles and responsibility in family & community;
6. visible increase on decrease in violence on women and girls;
7. responses to, changes in social customs like child marriage, dowry, discrimination against widows;
8. visible changes in women's participation level attending meeting, participating and demanding participation;
9. increase in bargaining and negotiating power at home, in community and the collective;

10. increase access to and ability to gather information;
11. formation of women collectives;
12. positive changes in social attitudes;
13. awareness and recognition of women's economic contribution within and outside the household;
14. women's decision-making over her work and income.

Quantitative indicators:

A. Demographic trends
   - maternal mortality rate
   - fertility rate
   - sex ratio
   - life expectancy at birth
   - average age of marriage

B. Number of women participating in different development programmers

C. Greater access and control over community resources/ government schemes-creche, credit cooperative, non formal education

D. Visible change in physical health status and nutritional level

E. Change in literacy and & enrollment levels

F. Participation levels of women in political process Monitorable targets for the Tenth Plan and beyond had certain key issues related to gender.
   - All children in school by 2003; all children to complete five years of schooling by 2007.
   - Reduction of gender gaps in literacy and wage rates by at least 50% by 2007.
   - Reduction of IMR to 45 per 1000 live births by 2007 and 28 by 2012.
   - Reduction of maternal mortality ratio (MMR) to 2 per 1000 live births by 2007 onto to by 2012.

India's declining sex ratio caused through foeticide, infanticide and systematic neglect requires urgent and comprehensive action. It is well evidenced that low literacy, endemic under nutrition and social inequality are closely related gender inequality is a crucial antecedent to endemic undernutrition.

Education:

Women's education is extremely important intrinsically as it is their human right and required for the flourishing of many of their capacities.

It is however, noticed that most programmes for education of girls and women in India have reinforced Gender roles specially motherhood in curriculum as well as impact evaluation. The huge study of nearly 94% of India's population done by Drez and others looks at female literacy and its negative and statistically significant impact on child mortality.

The questions of power are interlinked and we understand that what is necessary is both objective power in terms of economic resources, laws, institutional roles and norms held by others as well as subjective power in terms of self efficacy and entitlements. Empowerment of women is closely related to formal and informal sources of education. Late 19th century & 20th century reformers advocated women's education as a principal strategy to answer the 'women's question'. Many innovative efforts are accelerated after the NPE. In UP a renewal process of correcting gender stereotyping was initiated in 1998 looking at textbooks and training besides infrastructure and community mobilization. There is marked improvement in girls enrollment and steady decline in drop out rates.

Despite statistically positive trends closer studies show that privileged spaces in classrooms are occupied by boys. Girls are rarely addressed by their names. Girls sit in last rows in classes of mathematics and rarely muster courage enough to come close to the board where the teacher sits (usually a male in most remote areas? Private school initiative for gender concerns is rare Madarsas have large number of girls but like convents and Arya Kanya Pathshala's gender transformation is not their agenda. Moral science text books still have preponderance of men. Women as agents of social reform are not mentioned. CSO efforts have very often shown greater enhancement of girls self-esteem but in many cases there is poor cognitive development generally attributed to low paid, low qualified but highly motivated instructor. Kanya Vidya Dhan, free uniforms, mid-day meal, school attached creche, mothers meetings have all had positive results.

In various surveys conducted by ISST it has been apparent that parental apathy or opposition to girl child education is fast reading even in traditional male dominated states of north Indian. Given the right infrastructure-schools located in neighbourhoods, preferably with female teachers parents would allow girls to study "as long as they would like to". It may however be noticed as evidenced by researchers, the same families who are willing to see girls in college react violently if the girl decides to choose her partner in marriage or challenge other norms of feminine behavior.

Health:

2005-06 National Family Health Survey (NFHS -3) conducted through 18 research organizations between 2005 December and August 2006 provides us with several important data based insights not provided by earlier surveys. There has been a steady increase in institutional delivery percentages from NFHS - 1 to 3 from 26 to 41 the increase in rural from 17 to 31 is more promising than urban from 58 to 69. Overall fertility rate has declined from 3.4 to 2.7. The states of Punjab and Maharashtra have reached the replacement level of fertility, i.e. around 2 children per woman. Women in Chattisgarh and Orrissa are expected to have an average of about 2.5 children at current fertility rates. The urban areas in five states studied by NFHS, Chattisgarh, Gujrat, Maharashtra, Orissa and Punjab have reached below replacement level fertility. There is a difference between the fertility of women with no education and those with 10 or more years of schooling. Trends in antenatal care have remained more or less constant in NFHS - 1 and 2 between rural and urban women but have increased from 65 to 77% total. The five state study shows regional imbalances in post natal care from only 23 per cent in Chhatisgarh to 54-59 per cent in Maharashtra. Punjab and Gujrat.

More than 40% ever married women and about one third men in orissa and Gujrat are thin for their height, undernutrition is much lower in Punjab (12-14%) obesity is the major problem in Punjab 38% women are overweight. Overweight or obese women percentage has increased in the last 7 years from 16 to 20 per cent in Gujrat from 12 to 17 per cent in Maharashtra and from 4 to 7 per cent in Orissa. The extent of o verweight is greater ;n, women than men. Overall 14.8% women are obese. Except in Punjab ir. the other states more than 5) per cent of the children, of women without any education are underweight. The percentage of anaemia ranges from 38% in Punjab to 63% in Orissa. Anaemia prevalence is alarming among pregnant women 57.9 which is more than last recorded 49.7%. 33% of women still have BMI below normal, which has declined from 36.2. IMR has gone down. but gender differences persist. Tnis is true also of under 5 mortality. Life expectancy of women however stands a level higher than that of men. From 1961 to 2001 both in total population as well as in the population of 0-6 there has been a decline in sex ratio from 943 to 935 and 976 to 927 respectively. There is a fear that overall reduction cf state resources in the welfare sector and specially less than 1% investment it health is going to exacerbate the existing gender bias in society.

Political Participation:

Women's political participation has been considered a major measure of women's empowerment. Globally; through histories of the world we have records of very few regents, sovereigns; and active agents in nobility who were women. Champions of liberalism like John Stuart Mill had advocated women's participation in governance by the struggle for women suffrage in the self avowed liberal west very well illustrates the entrenched nature Of Patriarchical resistance to women's empowerment. in the last century more women heads of state could be counted in Asia as compared to Europe and the struggle for women suffrage in India was physically less violent but this is not reflective of greater acceptance of women in decision-making in public spaces.

To measure women's empowerment now GEM takes 3 indicators, women's participation in economic; political and professional activities. Within political power what is measured is mainly women in parliament, judiciary or in local bodies. Women's empowerment or disempowerment has to be seen in all areas physical, socio cultural religious, political legal and economic.

It is also now often pointed out that women's empowerment must be seen as a process where in we must consider women's awareness consciousness. choices with live alternatives, resources at their disposal, voice, agency and participation. These are all related to enhancement of women's capabilities and decisions they take individually or collectively for themselves.

Several programmes in India like Mahila Samakhya have accepted the process nature of women's empowerment. The understandings of empowerment in PACS has also been similar but planning of activity, time and budgets to ensure the empowering processes need greater scrutiny. Women's education, livelihood and personal exercise of agency have to be systematically promoted.

The 73rd and 74th Amendments of the Constitution have impacted nearly 600 million Indian people in 500,000 villages. Interestingly the percentage of women at various levels of political activity have risen from 4-5% to 25-40%. Both nationally as well as at the state and local levels women in elected bodies have been very few and even those who have been elected when observed from closer quarters present a complex picture. The money and muscle associated with the electoral process inhibits a large number of women from joining politics. Restriction on mobility, lack of control over resources and low literacy rates are well known obstacles but recent panchayat elections have evidenced a phenomenally large number of elected leaders much beyond reserved 33% seats. Areas where PACS, Mahila Samakhya or other CSO initiatives are working women. are more articulate and vigilant and have used opportunity to improve ICPS centres, primary schools sanitation and have also publicly dealt with issues of misbehavour with girls, violence and alcoholism as well as sensitive issues of widowed women dressing in coloured clothes. Women are increasingly demanding not only basis but also land literacy and fuller longer trainings instead of being short changed through orientations.

It is obvious that a more active Gram Sabha which is sensitive to women's specific issues is a much desired goal as a woman *sarpanch* or BDC member in a gender hostile *panchayat* may not be able to accomplish and sustain much for the benefit of women or the village community at large. More women in grass root organizations; better law and order will ensure better engagement of women in decision-making.

More than one million women have now entered political life in India and 43% of the seats are occupied by them district, province and national level. Women's participation is understood in terms of voter turn out, number of women contestants apart from the number of those who succeeded in winning.

In an interesting study sponsored by State Planning Commission in U.P. 2006 about 45% women both rural and urban reported being influenced by men of the family (father/ husband) in decision-making in the exercise of their ballot. 9 per cent reported external influence while 46 per cent exercise independent choice.

However, the battle to make the PRI's affective instruments of local rural governance is a battle, a struggle of the grass roots, population (women and men) against administrative apathy and listlessness, against ignorance and low awareness. For women these odds are accompanied and intermeshed with deep rooted patriarchal practices that determine and sanction norms of speech and behaviour both within and outside the home.

Thus while Pre election trainings of voluntary organisations and CSVOs serve to build awareness about the duties, responsibilities of PR's and about voting practices, the presence and working of women's voluntary organisations at the grass roots have served to sharpen women's understanding about the operation of patriarchy in personal lives and work. places and the methods and practices to overcome and combat them individually and collectively.

Organisations such as Mahila Samakhya working to conscientise and organise women in groups and sanghas are able to address the issue of women and their participation in a two fold manner. On the one hand they organise intensive training programmes for women PRI representatives to make them effective functionaries and on the other hand togethere own programmes with their members within there collectives serve to build a culture of questioning, critical thinking, collective decision-making and mobilisation, on public issues.

A mobilised community of women is thus able to raise issues of significance to the local community within the meetings, demand accountably from representatives and administrative officials regarding financial and procedural matters and intervene with creative suggestions.

It is thus that the dominance of patriarchy money power, party politics muscle power are steadily undercut and eroded and women's concerns are gradually pushed to the forefront of local politics.

Drawing from intensive discussions at the level of sanghas and mahasanghas and the experiences culled called from functionaries and from trainings, Mahila Samakhya has drawn out learnings to strengthen women's participation in the Panchayats. A memorandum incorporating these has been presented to the Panchayat Raj Department. It states-

- It is imperative to inscribe the budget for the village on the Panchayat Bhawan.
- There should be rules and strategies to train and activate women members who have been elected to the post of Pradhans or members.
- There should be strict rules for ensuring the participation of 2/3 voters in the open meeting.
- The signatures of the people in the executive register of the open meeting should be ensured.
- It should be compulsory for the Pradhan/Secretary to sit in the panchayat Bhawan.
- The development plan should be widely disseminated so that it can reach the general public.
- The dates and time of the panchayat meetings in the state of U.P. should be decided in advance.
- The venue of the meeting should be either the Panchayat Bhawan ofr a public place, to enable all gram sabha members to present their problems.

Thus it is apparent that women see effective and efficient functioning of panchayats closely linked to the issue of active women's participation. (Mahila Samakhya U.P. Annual Report 2004-05.

Entry into public space, utilisation of authority in practice, trainings by government and nongovernment agencies are all part of a process of gradual growth of knowledge, self-esteem and empowerment, which gives women the agency to function effectively in the political process.

Even proxy and dummy candidates may experience this process of empowerment women who stand and win from general seats are more likely to have a higher commitment towards, and an understanding of the political process.

Having a high participation of women at the local self government level can create an environment which is enabling for other women, receptive to the idea of gender based initiatives and can serve to monitor and implement community and gender based programmes of the government related to education, nutrition and health.

It offers a potential opportunity which can be utilised at an optimum level by appropriate trainings both capacity binding and information enhancing - by government departments and the NGO Sector.

Decision-Making:

In terms of decision-making NFHS il had reported in the rural areas women take 71% decisions regarding "what items to cook" 26% decisions regarding obtaining health care fro herself 10% in purchasing jewellery or other major household items. 12% decisions were taken by women with reference to staying with their parents or siblings and 37% about how to spend money; which they had earned. In the urban areas these figures were 71%, 35°%, 13%, 18% and 57% respectively. Women between ages 15 to 19 nearly 24% are not involved in any kind of decision-making only. 14% do not ask permission to go to the market. In rural sector 10% are involved with any decision-making and 74% need permission for going to the market. In urban sector however only 7% are not involved with any decisionmaking and 53% need permission for going to the market. Survey reports that of the 52% illiterate women 74% of urban resident and 55% of rural resident have access to money. Small studies on elected Panchayat leaders show episodic increase of their decision-making in personal, social and political spaces. Studies of the NFHS scale are necessary to retrieve such data specially in PACs programme areas. This could be done with reference to internal lending of SHG's as well as leveraging through: other agencies in terms of both economic status enhancement and their decision- making. Interestingly some studies reflect that women's working outside home in paid job does not always translate into appreciably greater autonomy within the household for most women. In a sample study at Sonipat and Noida 66% need to consult somebody and take permission before changing jobs. 27.6% women in Noida and 35.3% in Sonipat said they are allowed to buy nothing at all.

Working outside home women do believe that they have more experience (91.6%), enlarged social networks (48.3%) and stronger personality (32.2%) and an increased self esteem 985.3%) besides their decision-making power (62.2%). The researchers however observe that objective state of affairs do not bear this out and women's decision-making is concentrated to making small purchases. In buying and selling assets they have no say

Methodologically here there is a dilemma about privileging of perspective — that of the responmdent or that of the urban middle class educated researcher. This is particularly pertinent as the sense of being empowered is also importantly about "feeling empowered".

Self Help Groups:

PADS programme has largely utilized SHG's as an empowsering instrument. More than 80% of these are exclusively for women. The fifth national synthesis report

(Draft) reports that official perception has changed as SHG's are firmly raising voices and SHG's are being used to achieve RTI awareness:

- Women members are elected as PRI representatives.
- SHG/PRIs are regularly organising *Gram Sabha as a* forum for public appraisal.

Anecdotal accounts suggest that women are economically empowered those suffering domestic violence are given legal reference and awareness to prevent child marriage promote girls education and prevent dowry marriage and alcoholism.

Self-help groups have emerges as an important strategy for empowering women and alleviating poverty. SHG's are based on idea of dialogic small groups, which shall function at developing collective consciousness. !inked with micro credit these groups are able to access credit and subsidy to meet crisis needs as well as developmental needs reducing their dependence on money lenders. There is fair amount of evidence to suggest that PACs SHG's have successfully ensured people's entitlements including women.

Statistically PAC's initiatives in realizing entitlements show that - In Balika Samriddhi Yojana 189 females have been benefitted rfealizing 2572400 Rs. in Employment Guarantee Scheme 55397 women have been provided, 1271 girls enrolled and 9524 women provided Indira Awas Yojna. Kanya Vidya Dhan has been availed by 131 girls while Mahila Samridhi Yojana has benefitted 7 women. Maternity benefits have reached 2943 women and NFE educated 862 women. Old age pension went to 7774 women while no woman benefitted from the Pradhan Mantri Awas Yojna. Sam Vikas Yojna benefitted 975 women compared to 467 men Bridge courses benefitted 740 girls. Widow pension was ensured to 2948 women and 217 women get yellow cards.

The realization of entitlements has been primarily through RTI, NREGS and the women further train communities. in Jharkhand a large number of women were trained in social audit. In total number of beneficiaries of entitlement 13342 women in Bihar 156217 in Jharkhand 19906 women in Maharashtra 18762 in M.P. and Chhattisgarh and 55114 in U.P. were reached. Men have however benefitted more except in Bihar.

Violence:

The questions regarding crimes against women are most entrenched, as most of them are committed within the family NCRB records that the highest percdentage of crime against women is torture (37.7%) followed by Moleslation (22.4%); Rape (11.8%), Kidnapping (8.8%) and immoral traffic (3.7%). 4.6 Dowry Death and 6.5% eve teasing were recorded. the further details report that in victims of rape 532 were below 10 and 1090 below 14. 3189 within ages of 30-50. No age is safe for women. In U.P. nearly 32% crimes against women were committed within the family by husbands and relatives. This figure when compounded with 12% dowry deaths makes 45% of crimes domestically located. Incidents of honour killings and battery through not large are often threats to women's functioning and their emotional development is severely blighted. In caste ridden society women's caste membership increase her vulnerability. Small efforts to train police by UN agencies and state initiatives are encouraging but very small in scale. They require follow-ups and support monitoring.

Women and Work:

Women's work is statistically less visible non monetized and relegated to subsistence production and domestic side this accounts for 60% of unpaid family work and 98% of domestic work. The non paid work includes domestic chares like cocking, cleaning, child care aand care for the elderly and the handicapped-traditonally understood as women's work. Subsistence activities like pitches gardening post harvest processing, feeding farm hands, live stock maintenance, gathering of fuel, forest produce, unpaid family labour in family farm or enterprise are done by women who are reported to be non working housewives Census estimates 51.93% men & 25% women workers while NSS estimates 52.7 male and 25.68 female workers. Most men are in stable employment. Micro studies report many challenges - 20 out of 104 women reported in a survey as non working were actually winnowwwing, thrashing or paraboling (WB). S. Mukhopadhyaya in her study reports 4 times more work participation in her study. Female work participation rate in U.P. is reported as 11% with a Gender gap of 52% equal to. West Bengal but less than Punjab. 56% women are in community service 17% in Manufacturing & 8.6 rural women in agriculture. Only 4% women as against 10% men are in the formal sector. If women's work is rendered visible specially unpaid household work there will be many dramatic results Studies show that working women but 664 hours & others put 872 hours on child care, womens' share of work in 55% women's unpaid work is 51% while men's is 33%. R. Malathy's extrapolation estimates 23,773 core as the value of wowmen's household reserve rendered by women in the urban sector alone. From 17% women's contribution will increase to 33% of agricultural earning will include unpaid household work. Restriction on women's mobility, complete child care responsibility ideology of female seclusion, vulnerability to abuse, low access to information and mass media, low literacy, assumption that women's supplementary and confinement to largely manual untrained tasks leads to women's poor access to income.

Women and Reforms:

It is often argued that economic reforms have had a differential gender impact but there are further complexities. The reforms have meant more openness in trade regime and progressive decontrol of domestic production sector. There seems a steady withdrawal of state presence from the production sector arguing that this would promote greater efficiency and accountability. There has however been much protest that this will leave labour more vulnerable as profit motive alone drives the market. Market argue that since women are crowded towards the bottom end of labour market they will be more adversely impacted. The 55th round of National Sample Survey organization (1999-2000) generally reflects that over the years specially in urban areas gender differences in the structure of industrial and occupational distributions and distribution of labour status categories seems to have lessened. There is higher demand of female labour in some sectors which can be linked to a thrust towards export orientation and deregulation in the domestic production sector. According to Swapna Mukhopadhyaya changes in structure of job opportunities have not translated into overall reduction in the degree of market segmentation along gender lines. There is marginal decrease in employment of men and marginal increase for women in urban India. Educated women in the labour market who are unemployed are for more than their male counterparts 62.7% unemployed women in rural areas as compared to 56.9% men. It seems IT enabled sectors in recent years may have benefitted educated women. There is not enough reliable data but persistently low wages of women to the tune of 50% to 80% compare to men suggest systematic wage discrimination. Wage earnings in casual female workers in 1999-2000 were 64.70% of corresponding male earnings in rural India are even lower at 60.57% in urban India. 2005 HDR reports that women spend 457 minutes at work as compared to 391 minutes per day for men.

Ownership of Land:

A recent legislation of the Central Government, the Hindu succession Amendment Act 2005 has also moved towards women's equality in property rights. It makes Hindu women's inheritance rights in agricultural land legally equal to those of men. All daughters including married daughters age Co-parceners in joint family properly daughters now have the right to claim partition and to become 'Karta'. All daughters, married or unmarried can reside, seek partition of the parental dwelling place.

This law of the centre well have the power to displace any conflicting laws of the state which are unequal to women. this is a far reaching message to assure women control over property.

According to a recent study made by Bina Agarwal in Kerala, women's risk of physical violence from husbands is dramatically less of they own hand or a house. The incidence of violence is 49 per cent among women without property, but 18 per cent among land owning women and 7 per cent of they own both land and house.

Recent initiative of the state of U.P. (ordinance of 23 Feb. 2006) regarding the reduction of stamp duty on the purchase of land from 7 per cent 6 per cent has worked in the direction of more land being bought in the name of women in the family. This transfer of asset in favour of women though initially used by male members of the family to save family money will gradually contribute to build women's agency. 2,97715 transactions have been done in the name of women in 68 districts of Uttar Pradesh between April 2006 and August 2006. The women move out of their homes to sign the papers in Tehsils and in many cases it is their first exposure to an office. This initiative developed with women's trainings on legal, land and human rights literacy will go a long way.

However, this effectiveness is greatly linked with the willingness of the state administration to devolve effective administrative and financial power to the local self-governing units, and the responsiveness and sensitivity of the lower echelons of the administrative machinery to the aspiration and needs of the local population. Alcohol has not favoured women and increase in indirect taxes has also impacted them poorly. The thrust of budgets also seems to push people to private providers.

Government schemes could be seen as Relief policies like widow pension schemes. *Gender reinforcing assistance* like mother support schemes in health and *Empowering schemes for* women to demand and enjoy full human rights.

State Initiatives:

Development writers are so often used to repeating that focus of women development in India has shifted from 'welfare' in the 50's to development ir. the 70's and now to empowerment. This is hardly borne out in the programmes on the ground. There are largely schemes for relief like old age and widowhood schemes and major schemes related to Gender reinforcing assistance related to reproduction National Institute of Public Finance and Policy undertook the first gender budget exercise and categorized expenditure in 3 categories

National Institute of Public Finance & Policy Gender Analysis of the Budget

NIPFF undertook the first gender budget exercise and categorized expenditure n 3 categories.

1. Specifically targetted expenditure on women.
2. Pro women allocation - composite expenditure in the women component (at least 30%).
3. Mainstream expenditure with gender differential impact.

   It was understood that public expenditure can be clustered in terms of 4 categories:

   a) Protective and welfare services accounting for 67%
   b) Social service-education; water housing health 26%
   c) Economic resources-self employment training fuel supply management 4%

d) Regulatory services - awareness generation NCW 3%

Allocation for women directed scheme is pitiful. Only ten ministries/Departments have specially targetted schemes for women in India. The share of women specific programmes in departments like education, agriculture, tribal affairs and social justice is also only around one percent. No proper administrative mechanism for execution and monitoring of expenditure. Heads still under ruberic of benefits for mother and child. Shelter homes and counselling centres are still low on priority. NIPF observed that reduction in cost of foreign liquour has not positively impacted them.

It is, however, necessary that even though schemes are relief oriented the process of accessing them has often been an individual and collected struggle which has sometimes led to empowerment and at others disheartening. PACS strategy of collective pressure to access public resources for women has largely been empowering though anecdotal.

There are several critical issues to ensure a just an equitable state with reference to gender. Some issues are not addressable due to procedural limitations of data collection which makes specific recommendations difficult. There is need to develop a workable gender audit system for govt. & CSO programmes which would look at targets, training recruitments promotion, infrastructure and decision making opportunities. The verbal change from women welfare to women rights needs to be converted into reality. This has some direct fall outs. Pitiful allotment for Vriddha and Vidva Pension and minimum wages will have to be reconsidered in terms of living wages, recent work and human right to opportunities for highest form of physical and mental health.

Greatest inequity exits in family but poverty alleviation schemes address only the family. Just as one poverty calculation takes per capita consumption it should also address per capita income enhancement not family.

Gender budgets need participation of other departments besides the existing ones. Gender auditing of all organizations is necessary.

As is evidenced in many studies level of awareness of government schemes is very low so more effective publicity is necessary. A more effective MIS system for monitoring women welfare, women empowerment programmes is to be developed which is simple, transparent and involves both government and non government functionaries. Gender resource centres with autonomy need to be established in all states and in case of larger states there must be more than one such centre involving academic & activities.

Practically no schemes exist to encourage women in non stero typical occupations. Training of women in leadership market research and entrepreneurship with follow ups must be institutionalized. At the national as well as state levels we need a full fledged mechanism to ensure gender sensitive policy, implementation through a participatory apex body. Clearer definition of work, Joint Pattas for women & men will ensure better control of women over resources as well as their acknowledgement in National income. Country's inclusive agenda requires a consistent engendering at all levels.

Perception of Women Empowerment in India

Women constitute almost 50% of the world's population. As per as their social status is concerned, they are not treated as equal to men in all the places. Empowering may be understood as enabling people, especially women to acquire and possess power resources, in order to make decision on their own or resist decisions that are made by others that affect them. A person may said to be powerful when he/she has control over a large portion of power resources in society. The extent of possession of various resources such as personal wealth, such as land skills, education, information, knowledge, social status, position held, leadership capabilities of mobilization.

It is now widely believed that empowerment of women i.e., providing equal rights, opportunities and responsibilities to women, will go a long way in removing the existing gender discrimination. Women empowerment in contemporary Indian society in forms of their work, education, health and media images in the forms of their work, education, health and media images in the context of lineage; rule of residence and household chores, their context of lineage, rule of residence and household chores, their participation in social and political activities, their legal status in terms of marriage, divorce and inheritance of property, seeking wealth care should be taken into consideration. Empowerment in terms of knowledge and awareness of ones own life and society including legal, raise their status with regarded to the lives. While empowerment deals with her or his expectation arising out of the situation. Similarly, a role deals with duties and obligation, empowerment deals with rights. For instance, it is commonly assumed that the most is a woman, a wife a cook, a teacher of her children and daughter-in-law and so on.

Women constitute almost 50% of the world's population. As per as their social status is concerned, they are not treated as equal to men in all the places, through in the western countries women are treated on par with men in most of the fields, their counterpart in the east suffers from many disabilities.

The disabilities on the one hand and the inequalities between men and women on the other, have given rise to what is known "Gender problem". All the world and particularly in South and East Asia and Africa the gender problem has assumed importance during the recent years the gender issue has become virtually a crucial point of argument. It is now widely believed that empowerment of women i.e., providing equal rights, opportunities and responsibilities to women, will go a long way in removing the existing gender discrimination. Women empowerment in contemporary Indian society in forms of their work, education, health and media images in the forms of their work, education, health and media images in the context of lineage, rule of residence and household chores, their context of lineage, rule of residence and household chores, their participation in social and political activities, their legal status in terms of marriage, divorce and inheritance of property, seeking wealth care should be taken into consideration. Empowerment in terms of knowledge and awareness of ones own life and society including legal raise their status with regarded to the lives.

Before thinking about the empowerment of women, one needs to understand the exact meaning of the word empowerment. According to Cambridge English Dictionary empowerment means "to authorize". In the context of the people they have to be authorized to have control over their lives. When applied in the context of development the particular segment of population, the poor, the women, the vulnerable, the weak, the oppressed and the discriminated have to be "empowered" to have control over their lives to better their socioeconomic and political conditions.. But the questions raised are, who empowers them and how to empower them? Ideally speaking no one empowers any one. the best way is 'self empowerment', by the segments of population mentioned above are handicapped both structurally and culturally to empower themselves without any outside help and affirmative action by the State and others. But still as long as these segments of population do not make any effort at self-employment. it would be long and arduous task and process for the outsiders to empower them.

The principal of gender equality was recognized in the United Nations Charter in 1945 and the UN Declaration of

Human Rights in 1948, the majority of development planners did not fully address the role of wornen in development process. In 1975, the first UN Conference of Women and Development was held at maxico city under the motto; "Equality, Development and peace". The need to integrate women into development was internationally proclaimed in the 1995 Bering Conference. The Economic. Survey (1999-2000) used an entire section on gender inequaiity. It began with a reminder of the commitment grade in the ninth plan document of allocating 30 per cent of resources for women's development schemes through "Women's Component Plans".

According to Menon and Probhu (2001), there was a strong plea for investing in women's equality on the ground that this made economic sense and spoke of "the social rate of return on investment In women" being greater that the corresponding rate for men.

According to Paten (2002), women's development can be attained by improving here status and bargaining power in the economy.

Sushma Sachay (1998) argues that approaches and strategic for women empowerment could be possible by outlining the mechanisms and tools that till influence for women empowerment. Decisions making process, multidimensional process that are enable worn to realize their full identity and powers in all walks of life.

Empowering may be understood as enabling people, especially women to acquire and possess power resources, in order to make decision on their own or resist decisions that are made by others that affect them. A person may said to be powerful when he/she has control over a large portion of power resources in society. The extent of possession of various resources such as personal wealth, such as land skills, education, information, knowledge, social status, position held, leadership trains, capabilities of mobilization.

The National Policy on Education (1986) suggested certain strategies to empower women. Accordingly, women become empowered through collective reflections and decision making enable them to become agency of social change. The global conference on Women Empowerment (1988), highlighted empowerment as the best way of making own partners in development the development of women and children in Rural Areas (DWCRA) program was initiated as a sub scheme of the national wide poverty alleviation program i.e., the Integrated Rural Development Program (IRDP). It aims at imparting selfreliance to rural areas through income generating skill s along with group organization skills. Keeping this in view the year 2001 was celebrated as "The Women's Empowerment Year". Human resource development and empowerment of women unlock the door for modernization of society,. Instated of remaining as passive beneficiaries, women must become active partner. Participation and control over resources of power are considered as the critical indicators in the process of development discharged women especially in rural areas, possess the least proportion of these resources and as a result they are powerless and dependent on the powerful and wealthy.

We will now realize the vital importance of the terms such as role, empowerment and function for an understanding of society. These terms tell us how individual and groups organize themselves as well as relate to each other. Very simple, role tells us about what is expected from individuals in a particular situation. While empowerment deals with her or his expectation arising out of the situation. Similarly, a role deals with duties and obligations wile empowerment deals with rights. For instance, it is commonly assumed that the most is a women, a wife a cook; a teacher of her children and daughter-in-law and so on. What happens when the mother is also the principal of the local village school? Not only does she have to deal with a range of roles and empowerments, but also with he tensions that may raise out of her ole s mother and her role as an administrator.

"Woman reposes more closely on the central surface of life, while man hunts it in the boundaries of existence, always concerned to overcome, and in the last analysis, to kill. A woman has a secret alliance with eternal life and man with the principle of death. Woman wants to embrace the contradiction of life and to reconcile them in the act of degree so. Man on the other hand release the tension between opposites by annihilating one of the sides, the one he finds unpleasant. He seeks the solution not in love and reconciliation, but in over coming and annihilation. He has a militant and not an erotic manner.

The male principle borne of isolation, makes solitude thermal, seeks being n itself and disturbs life as a wholes his being is battle and self service, his will- to-life is concerned with ascertaining his own person or overthrowing that of the stranger until the motive of salvation kindles with in him. Woman with her sustaining constitutions is at one and is harmony with the basis of the world. But man wants to change the world to bring it forward to overcome it".

Contemporary Indian society has been exposed to the broad processes of social transformation, agricultural modernization and economic development urbanization and globalization. However, these processes have generated regional imbalances, sharpened class inequalities and augmented the gender disparities. Hence, women have become critical symbols of these growing imbalances. All these have affected adversely the various aspects of women's empowerment in the contemporary Indian society.

The family and women's work is not enough to say that any society consists of men and women. It is equally important to look at how the two groups of people interact, as well as at the role and exceptions each group has of the other. Such roles and exceptions are a product of the stereotypes of each gander. By gender, stereotype we mean attributes and qualities commonly associated with a gender.

Thus, the first idea on gender role differences, which a child acquires, is that of women of one's family marrying and leaving their homes to leave with different groups of people. Secondly, men appear to exercise far greater influence in decision making and are tar more visible and audible than their wives. Third most of the tasks within the home are done by the mother, grand mother, sisters and so on. At meal times they carry food to the fields for the men. All these tasks, which consume time and energy, are not counted as work and there is no payment involved. In western countries, women's groups; politicians and other concerned individuals have been arguing for payment for house work and childcare. In India, the question of payment for household jobs has not really been an important issue or demand. As we shall see, there are many other issues, which require urgent attention. At the same time, it is important for us to remember that non-payment should not also mean non-recognition. The fact that women. are expected to perform all these tasks as a part of their conventional roles and on special merit is awarded to them for these tiring and tiresome jobs.

As per to 1981 figures 19.7 per cent Indian women were recorded as paid workers. Of whom over 87 per cent were in the unrecognized or informal sector of the economy. The work participation rate woman in 1991 and 2001 was 22.3 and 25.7 per cent respectively. The increase in the work participation of women during the decade 1991-2001 is mainly due to the increase in the proportion of marginal workers (6.3 per cent io 11 per cent) in total female work force. It is held by many observation of Indian economy that without women's paid or unpaid labour the Indian agricultural economy would not be able to function. In the informal sector, there is no legal redressal for problems; no maternity or other leave benefits and little security of service. Working long hours as domestic servants, stitching clothes for the garment export industry, working on the assembly line of small electronics manufacturing units or the beedi, tobacco. cashew nut factories. A woman lives in fear of retrenchment, exploitation and low wages.

According to Maithreyi Krishna Raj that though women were concerned about continuing their jobs, they were not looking for better prospects nor have they begun with a long-range carrier strategy. Once in a job, women rarely attempted to acquire further qualifications was by no means clear-cut. T.S. Papola's study of workingwomen, which covered a range from those in supervisory post in industrial establishments to unskilled workers, showed that women were more different than men in respect of their promotion prospects.

Papol's study showed that women were discriminated against at the time of promotions tended to be crowded into lower status electrical and primary school jobs. They were rarely promoted to executive and supervisory posts. As regards employment and promotion to supervisory category, male employers defend themselves by pointing out that women did not come forth to be recruited or promoted.

In the urban areas, the working class, and men in particular have a wide range of job options available to them. The study by Leela Kasturi shows that when unemployed weavers from Tamil Nadu migrant to Delhi, the women folk found jobs only as domestic servants. While men become mechanics, cooks or drivers. The shift in residence meant a severance with an established way of life and the support of the extended family.

For the majority of working class women, a job is essential. In relation to the limited chances for occupational mobility, when men and women work in the same occupation, female tasks are often the more arduous and time consuming. For instance, in paddy cultivation they spend long hours in sowing, weeding transplanting. In Kerala the extraction of the cashew seed from a corrosive liquid is women's work.

Again when both sexes do identical jobs, women often get paid less than man. Protests are rare, apart from ignorance of legal and other rights; there is a fear of exploitation and sexual harassment by the landlord or contractor.

Irrespective of social class there is at the level of belief, widespread commitment to the nation that a women's job just not interfere or compete with her primary role of wife and mother. There is also concern with her physical safety and the respectability of the occupation. Clearly, working class familiar are far less able to ensure circumstances.

NGO's SHGs have been working to promote women more viable towards social, political, economic and cultural development micro finance is a significant factor and accessible to small and micro enterprises, socio-economic progress of poor women. Education and training also plays a major role in changing the life of poor women. The several institutions have been extending all types of vocational training, income generating activities and self-employment activities for poor women.

Empowerment of women is mainly related to their participation in decision-making with regard to raising and distribution of resources i.e., income, investments and expenditures at all levels. Even though the Government of Karnataka has formulated and implemented various schemes of the social economic and overall development of the rural women, when the present position of women is taken into account these schemes do not appear effective in enhancing the confidence and capability of the women.

Empowering the poor women in rural areas to sustain their surrounding ecology is a necessity not only to stoop the ecological degradation but also for the physical survival of poor people. Almost every village in India has what is called "Common Property Resources (CDPs). Common Property Resources can be defined as "those resources, which are exploited by all people in the village free of cost by expending their labour.

8

Women Empowerment and Development

The empowerment of women is one of the central issues in the process of development of countries all over the world. Tamil Nadu has a glorious tradition of recognizing the importance of empowering women over -several centuries now. The contribution of writers and social reformers has been well documented. The Government of India has made Empowerment of Women as one of the principal objectives of the Ninth Five Year Plan (1997-2002) and also declared 2001 as the year of '*Women's Empowerment*'. These issues of gender equality are discussed in World Conferences, National and International Conferences, etc. Our Constitution has conferred and guaranteed equality before law, universal adult franchise and equal opportunities for men and women as fundamental rights. The imperative of gender partnership in matter of development has been recognised. In order to give a fillip to empowerment of women and appropriate institutional mechanisms and interventions have been consciously built into the development design. Separate institutions for women and child development, departments at the Central and State levels, creation of the National Commission for Women and also State Commission for Women in several States are some of the important developments for the betterment and prosperity of women.

The launching of Rashtriya Mahila Kosh, Indira Mahila Yojana, Mahila Samridhi Yojana, reserving of onethird of the number of seats in Panchayats and the local bodies are programmes launched with a view to improve and empower women socially, economically and in political frontiers.

Concept of Empowerment of Women:

Empowerment is a multi-faceted, multi-dimensional and multi-layered concept. Women's empowerment is a process in which women gain greater share of control over resources - material, human and intellectual like knowledge, information. ideas and financial resources like money - and access to money and control over decision-making in . the home, community, society and nation, and to gain 'power'. According to the Country Report of Government of India, *"Empowerment means moving from a position of enforced powerlessness to one of power".*

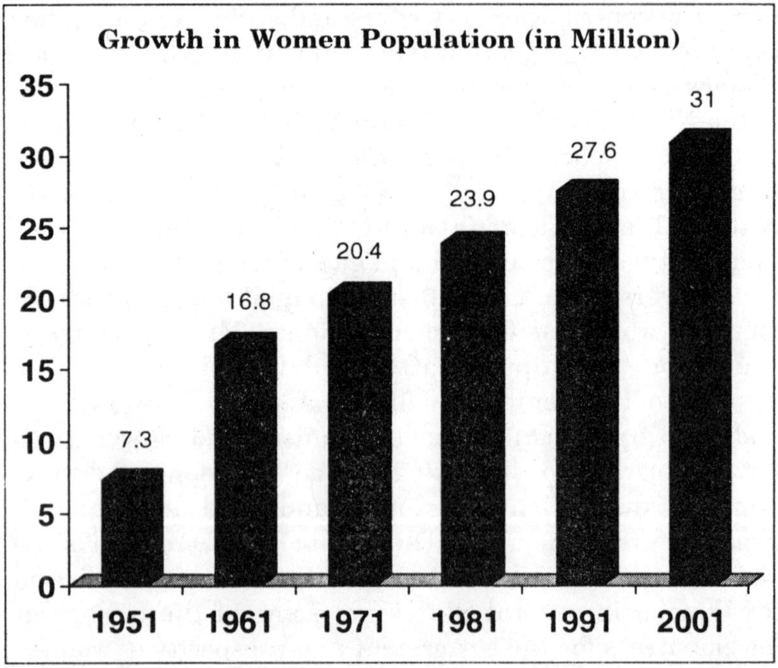

Status of Women in Tamil Nadu: Demographic features:

Tamil Nadu's population growth has been stabilized and growing slowly over the years, thanks to the welfare measures taken by the Government. Female population constitutes nearly half of the total population in the State. The status of women with regard to population over five decades is given in Table -1.

Table -1: Growth in Women Population

(in million)

Census Years	Tamil Nadu			All India		
	Male	Female	Persons	Male	Female	Persons
1951	22.8	7.3	30.1	186	175.6	361.1
1961	16.9	16.8	33.7	226	212.9	439.2
1971	20.8	20.4	41.2	284	264.1	548.2
1981	24.5	23.9	48.4	353	330.0	683.3
1991	28.3	27.6	55.9	439	407.1	846.3
2001	31.4	31.0	62.4	531	495.7	1027.0

Source: Directorate of Census Co-operations, Tamil Nadu.

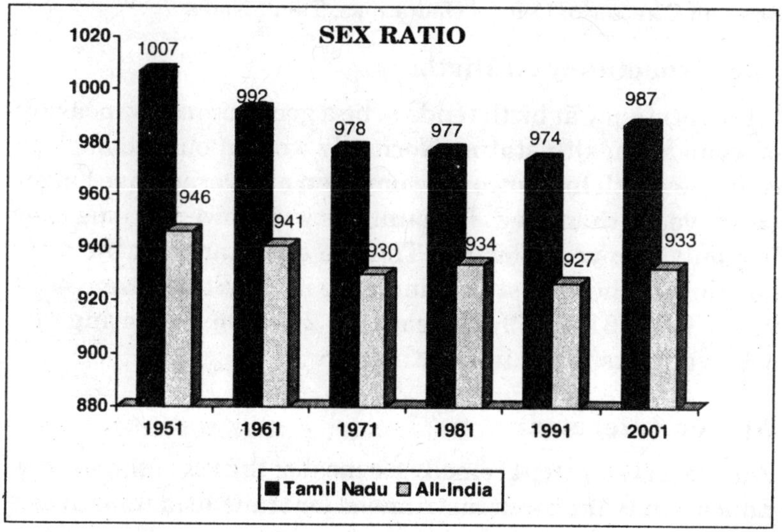

Sex Ratio:

Sex ratio, (i.e.) the number of female per thousand males - is a significant indicator of the status of women. In Tamil Nadu, the ratio has registered a continuous decline except in 2001. According to the 2001 Population Census, the sex ratio for the State stood at 987 as against 974 in 1991 Census. The rural sex ratio is relatively favourable at 992 compared to 981 in urban areas. It may also be noted that sex ratio in Tamil Nadu was consistently better than all-India average. The following table depicts the sex ratio in Tamil Nadu and All - India.

Table-2: Sex Ratio in Tamil Nadu and All-India

Year	Tamil Nadu	All-India
1951	1007	946
1961	992	941
1971	978	930
1981	977	934
1991	974	927
2001	987	933

Source: Director of Census Operations, Tamil Nadu.

Life Expectancy At Birth:

Life expectancy at birth tends to be a good summary measure of women's health status. Normally women outlive men. In countries with high income women on an average live longer by six years than men. In countries with lower income they live only two years longer. The life expectancy at birth for female has shown a steady increase in the State, from 39.74 years in 1961 to 69.75 years in 2001-06 reflecting the achievements made in health sector.

Women Literacy:

Education is a potent remedy for most of the ills of the society. Education is the main instrument for transformation in any society. The economic and social returns to education for women are substantial. By educating its women, a country can reduce poverty, improve productivity, ease population pressure and offer its children a better future. A ***'package approach'*** *is* required for developing female education.

There is a wide disparity between male and female literacy rates. As per 2001 Census, the literacy rate was

Female Literacy Rate in Tamil Nadu - 2001 Census

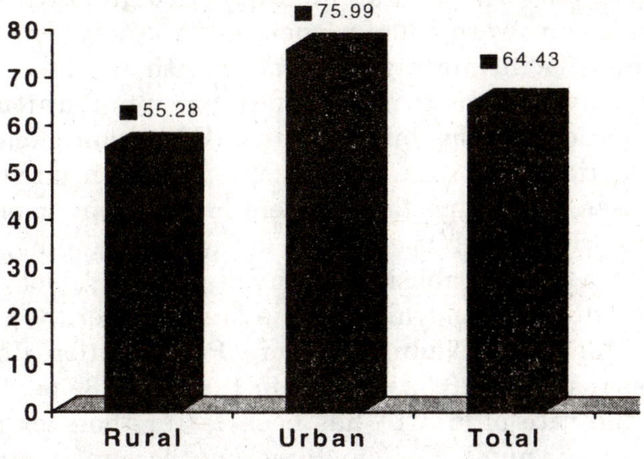

64.4 per cent and 82.4 per cent for females and males respectively in the State. There also exists a rural-urban gender divide in literacy rate across Tamil Nadu. The rate was 76 for urban female where as it was 55 per cent for its rural counterparts. Compared to urban female literacy rates, the rural rate was lower by 20.71 percentage points, where as the percentage point difference among males in urban and rural areas was only 11.82. The differences in the levels of literacy between males and females was significantly higher in rural areas than in urban areas. This indicates that specific intervention may be required for developing the literacy rates of the female population especially (less privileged classes) in rural areas.

Table -3: Female Literacy Rate in Tamil Nadu - 2001 Census

Region	*Male*	*Female*	*Persons*
Rural	77.15	55.28	66.21
Urban	88.97	75.99	82.53
Total	82.42	64.43	73.45

Source: *Director of Census Operations, Tamil Nadu.*

Employment and Work Participation Rate:

The work participation rate indicates to a great extent the economic empowerment of women in the society. The status of women is intimately connected with their economic position, which in turn depends on opportunities for participation in economic activities. Education along with participation of women in workforce has been universally recognised as an important element in the adoption of small family norms, which is essential for family planning. There has been a considerable improvement in the entry of women in all sectors of employment in the State. As per the Census results for Tamil Nadu, the Work Participation Rate for females rose from 26.52 per cent in 1981 to 31.32 per cent in 2001, the rate of growth has been faster than for males. However, the number of female workers accounted for 34.72 per cent in the total workforce of 278 lakhs in 2001. The corresponding figure for 1991 Census was 34.06 per cent. In the total population, nearly half were females but they accounted for only 34 per cent of the total workers. This proportion has to be improved for ensuring better and all round economic empowerment. Table-4 shows the Work Participation Rate as well as number of workers in Tamil Nadu.

Women and Political Participation:

Political equality to all children regardless of birth, sex, colour, etc. is one of the basic premises of democracy. Political equality includes not only equal right to franchise but also more importantly, the right to access to the institutionalised

Table -4: Work Participation Rates and Number of Workers in Tamil Nadu (Census based)

Variable	WPR (%)			No. of Workers (lakhs)		
	1981	1991	2001	1981	1991	2001
Rural						
Male	59.24	58.28	59.38	96.7	108.2	104.0
Female	33.55	38.50	41.33	54.1	70.1	71.8
Persons	46.48	48.49	50.39	150.8	178.3	175.8
Urban						
Male	51.25	52.78	56.37	41.8	51.4	77.6
Female	11.97	13.10	18.42	9.3	12.2	24.8
Persons	32.05	33.34	37.59	51.1	63.6	102.4
Total						
Male	56.58	56.39	58.96	138.5	159.6	181.6
Female	26.52	29.89	31.32	63.4	82.4	96.6
Persons	41.73	43.31	44.78	201.9	241.9	278.2

Source: *Census 1981, 1991 & 2000, GOI.*

centres of power. Thus, political participation of women means not only using the right to vote but also power sharing, co-decision making and co-policy making at all levels. The active participation of women in political sphere is integral to empowerment of women and helps to build a gender-equal society as well as to speed up the process of national development. Women's political empowerment is premised on three fundamental and non-negotiable principles: (a) the equality between women and men; (b) women's right to the full development of their potentials; and (c) women's right to self-representation and self-determination. In PRI women are increasingly coming to the fore and are providing leadership at the grass root level. This has profound social implications which gives a long way in addressing gender related discrimination in development.

Gender Equality Index (GEI) in Tamil Nadu:

GEI measurers the human development attainments of females as a percentage over that of males. The Gender

Equality Index for Tamil Nadu reflects that the status of women in Tamil Nadu had considerably improved between 1981 and 1991. Among the 15 major States in India, Tamil Nadu stood second in GEI in 1991 thanks to the huge investments in the areas of education and health sectors. This summary measure indicates that the gender bias in Tamil Nadu is very low compared to all-India and other major States (Table - 5).

Gender Development Index (GDI):

GDI is the touchstone of the position of women in society. The GDI (2001) for Tamil Nadu is 0.654. GDI values for the districts in Tamil Nadu vary from 0.766 in Chennai to 0.582 in Dharmapuri and Villupuram. The status of women was the lowest in Dharmapuri in terms of literacy rate, enrolment ratio and Life Expectancy at Birth which are reflected in low GDI (Table-6).

Table -5: Gender Disparity Index: Major States

States	1981		1991	
	Value	Rank	Value	Rank
Andhra Pradesh	0.744	2	0.801	3
Assam	0.462	14	0.575	12
Bihar	0.471	13	0.469	14
Gujarat	0.723	4	0.714	6
Haryana	0.526	12	0.714	6
Karnataka	0.707	6	0.753	5
Kerala	0.872	1	0.825	1
Madhya Pradesh	0.664	8	0.662	9
Maharashtra	0.740	3	0.793	4
Orissa	0.547	11	0.639	10
Punjab	0.688	7	0.710	7
Rajasthan	0.650	9	0.692	8
Tamil Nadu	0.710	5	0.813	2
Uttar Pradesh	0.447	15	0.520	13
West Bengal	0.556	10	0.631	11
All India	0.620	-	0.676	-

Source: *National Human Development Report, 2001.*

The table below exhibits the district-wise HDI and GDI values of the State.

Table-6: District-wise HDI and GDI Values, 2001

District	HDI Value	GDI Value
Chennai	0.757	0.766
Kancheepuram	0.712	0.710
Thiruvallur	0.654	0.651
Cuddalore	0.644	0.643
Villupuram	0.587	0.582
Vellore	0.658	0.655
T.V. Malai	0.612	0.608
Salem	0.626	0.625
Namakkal	0.636	0.631
Dharmapuri	0.584	0.582
Erode	0.658	0.656
Coimbatore	0.699	6.697
The Nilgiris	0.685	0.686
Trichi	0.671	0.671
Karur	0.647	0.641
Perambalur	0.596	0.592
Thanjavur	0.630	0.629
Nagapattinam	0.654	0.652
Thiruvarur	0.637	0.633
Pudukkottai	0.618	6.615
Madurai	0.661	0.661
Theni	0.628	0.628
Dindigul	0.641	0.638
Ramanathapuram	0.629	0.626
Virudhunagar	0.651	0.649
Sivagangai	0.640	0.635
Tirunelveli	0.658	0.656
Thoothukudi	0.703	0.703
Kanniyakumari	0.711	0.708
Tamil Nadu	0.657	0.654
All India	0.571	0.553

Source: *Tamil Nadu Human Development Report, State Planning Commission..*

The comparison between the two shows that if the GDI rank is less than the HDI value in a district, the position of women in that district is very poor compared to men. If the GDI is greater than HDI, there will be greater gender equality in human development. *In* terms of GDI Chennai is well placed, followed by Nilgiris, where the GDI is higher than HDI. In the districts of Tiruchy, Madurai, Theni and Thoothukudi, the HDI and GDI are found to be the same, indicating absence of gender inequality. In the district of Dharmapuri though the GDI is the lowest, in relative terms it is lower in Karur, Villupuram, Namakkal and Sivagangai, where the differences between HDI and GDI is higher. Compared to all-India, the gender bias is very low in Tamil Nadu.

Strategies Adopted by Government of Tamil Nadu for Women Empowerment:

It was recognised that the main obstacles to empowerment has been the low level of educational attainments as well as poverty among women. Taking into account this fact, the Government of Tamil Nadu have framed various policies, designed specific interventions *and* implemented many programmes to eradicate poverty and to provide education to the vulnerable sections of the society.

Education of Women:

Education to women is the most powerful instrument of changing their position in the society. Education also brings about reduction in inequalities and also acts as a means to improve their status within the family. In order to encourage education of women at all levels and to dilute gender bias in the provision and acquaintance of education, schools, colleges and even universities were established exclusively for women in the State. To bring more girl children, especially from marginalized BPL families, into the main stream of education, Government has been providing a package of concessions in the form of free supply of books, uniform, boarding and lodging, clothing for hostilities, mid-day meals, scholarships, free by-cycles and so on. The Mother Teresa Women University has been established for the development of Women Studies and to encourage higher education among women and their social mobility.

Periyar EVR Nagammai Scheme:

Periyar EVR Nagammai Free Education Scheme has been implemented in the State from 1989-90 to women students irrespective of caste, creed and community to encourage their education and to reduce dropout rate. As per the scheme those students' whose parental annual income is less than Rs.24,000/- are exempted from payment of tuition fees in under - graduate courses. During 2005-06, 8936 women students were benefited under this scheme. In 2006-07, a sum of Rs.65.00 lakhs has been allocated for this scheme.

Free Coaching Exclusively for Women Students:

To encourage and enable the women students to appear for the IAS/IPS examinations, the Government established two free coaching centers -one at Queen Mary's College, Chennai and the other at Arulmigu Meenakshi Government College for Women, Madurai. In each center, 60 women students are being given free coaching. During the current year, the government has provided a sum of Rs.1.00 lakh for implementing this scheme.

Entrepreneurship Awareness Programme (EAP):

In order to empower women, Science city has been organising Entrepreneurship Development Programme (EDP) and Entrepreneurship Awareness Programme (EAP) to bring out the talents of women and to make them stand on their own feet. To ascertain the status of women scientists, Science city has embarked upon the task of creating a data-base of women scientists in the entire State of Tamil Nadu. To encourage the women scientists, Science city has instituted Life Time Achievement Award and Young Women Scientist Awards. During 2005, five women scientists were awarded the Young Women Scientists Award.

Tamil Nadu Corporation for Development of Women:

Tamil Nadu Corporation for development of women was established in 1983 which aims at the socio-economic empowerment of women. As a prelude, the Corporation is implementing the Mahalir Thittam among poor rural women to promote saving habits, nurture entrepreneurial skills and aptitudes, promote exposure to banking transactions and to free them from the clutches of local moneylenders. The scheme is being implemented in partnership with Non-Governmental Organisations (NGOs) and Banks. Under the scheme, SHGs are formed and monitored through NGOs affiliated with the Tamil Nadu Corporations for Development of Women, Ltd.

Self Help Groups:

Self Help Groups are small homogenous groups consisting of 12-20 women from BPL families voluntarily organised to promote savings. They are self-managed groups of poor women which primarily came into existence to mobilise financial resources through their own savings and lend the same amongest themselves to meet the credit needs of their members. The specific objectives of SHGs are to:

- improve saving habits among women;
- increase the total family income;
- fulfill the economic needs through self-employment of women;
- utilise bank loan and government welfare schemes;
- help the members to escape from the clutches of moneylenders; and
- mobilise financial resources.

The SHG movement has emerged as a powerful and vibrant movement spread over the length and breadth of the State. As on 30.6.2006 there were 3,19,713 SHGs under Mahalir Thittam with a total savings of Rs.1,127.89 crones in Tamil Nadu. The position of this vibrant movement is depicted below:

Table -7: Status of SHGs in Tamil Nadu

Particulars	Status
Total number of SHGs	3,19,713
Total number of Group Members (lakhs)	51.68
Number of Rural Groups	2,62,270
Number of Rural Group Members	42,68,195
Number of Urban Group	57,443
Number of Urban Group Members	9,00,067
Total Savings (Rs. in crones)	1127.89
Credit Linked Groups	2,29,562
Amount of Loan disbursed (Rs. in crones)	1837.61

Source: *Policy Note, Rural Development Department, 2006-07.*

Capacity Building and Skill formation:

In order to improve the entrepreneurial ability and skill of the women, Government has been imparting various types of training designed to promote self and wage employment.

Skill Up-gradation Training Programme:

Provision of skill training to women in SHG has been given recognition so as to enable them to start their own income generating activities. The duration of the training and the cost depends on the nature of the trade selected by the members. Till March 2006, 60957 women have been provided skill training. The Government have proposed to train another 23000 women in 2006-07.

Entrepreneurship Development Training Programme for Women (EDP)

EDP training is conducted by TNCDW to expose the SHG women to various business opportunities and to motivate them to start economic activities. Up to March 2006, the Corporation has trained 6,34,991 women in co-ordination with other Government departments such as Rural Development, Agriculture, Industries and Commerce, Backward Classes, TAHDCO, Slum Clearance Board, etc. In 2006-07, 22000 more SHG women will be provided EDP Training by TNCDW.

Women Empowennent in India

Throughout history and in many societies including India, gender inequality was part and parcel of an accepted male-dominated culture. Atrocities and discrimination are the two major problems, which the Indian women face in the present day society. The traditional mentalities of India assume that the place of women is mainly concentrated to the household activities like kitchen work and upbringing of the children. They have been considered as the sexobject and inferior to the men in different spheres of knowledge. The 'Sati Pratha', Pardah System', 'Child Marriage', 'Dowry System', etc. have been some form of atrocities and discruninatory attitudes against the women.

Even after fiftyseven years of Indian independence, women are still one of the most powerless and marginalized sections of Indian society. The 2001 Census shows that the sex ratio for India is 933, which is lowest in the world. Percentage of female literacy is 54.16 (2001 Census) against male literacy of 75.85 per cent. In India, women's representation in Parliament and in the State Assemblies has never beyond 8 and 10 per cent respectively. Most of the working women remain outside the organised sector. A mere 2.3 per cent women are administrators and manages, 20.5 per cent professional and the technical workers all of whom collectively earn 25 per cent of the shared income. Violence against women is on the rise.

The democratic process in India created the awareness among the women about their plightful condition. The principle of gender equality is enshrined in the Indian Constitution in its Preamble, Fundamental Rights, Fundamental Duties and Directive Principles. The Constitution not only grants equality to women, but also empowers the state to adopt measures of positive discrimination in favour of women. The 73rd and 74th Amendments (1993) to the Constitution of India provided for reservation of seats (at least one-third) in the local bodies of Panchayats and Municipalities for women. Another Constitutional Amendment (84th Constitutional Amendment Act 1998) reserving 33 per cent seats in Parliament and State Legislatures is in the pipeline.

The Indian Government has passed various legislations to safeguard Constitutional rights to women. These legislative measures include, the Hindu Marriage Act (1955), The Hindu Succession Act (1956), Dowry Prohibition Act (1961), Medical Ternnination of Pregnancy Act (1971), Equal Remuneration Act (1976), Child Marriage Restraint Act (1976), Immoral Trafficking (Prevention) Act (1986) and finally Pre-natal Diagnostic Technique (Regulation and Prevention of Measure) Act (1994) etc.

Apart from these, various welfare measures have been taken up by the Government from time to time to empower to the women. They are, the support to Training for - Employment Programme (1987), Mahila Samriddhi Yojana (1993), the Rashtriya Mahila Kosh (1992-93), Indira Mahila Yojana (1995), DWACRA Plan (1997) and Balika Samriddhi Yojana (1997). On 12th July, 2001, the Mahila Samriddhi Yojana and Indira Mahila Yojana have been merged into the integrated self-help group programme i.e. Swayam Siddha:

The Government of India in 1953 established a Central Social Welfare Board with a nation-wide programme for grants-in-aid for women, children and under-privileged group. A separate department of women and child development was set up at the Centre in 1985 to give a distinct identity and provide a nodal point on matters relating to women's development. National Commission on women was created by an Act of Parliament in 1992. Besides these, India has also ratified various international conventions and human rights instruments committing to secure equal rights of women. Key among them is the ratification of the Convention of Elimination of All Forms of Discrimination Against Women (CEDAW) in 1991

The emancipation of women is not a simple matter. It requires the attitudinal change of the husband, other family members and society as a whole to the women. The community consciousness and bureaucratic efforts are integral parts of the implementation of the programmes. The

Shri Nagendra Kumar Pradhan, Minister, School & Mass Education inaugurating the state-level 103rd Birth Anniversary function of Latc Nabakrushna Choudhury held at Jayadev Bhavan on 23.11.2004.

Siddhartha Dash is a Gold Medalist, Post-Graduate in Political Science, also having an M.Phil degree and resides at Qrs.-3R-9/2, 2, Unit-9 Flats, Bhubaneswar.

first and foremost priority should be given to the education of women, which is the grassroot problem. The struggle for gender justice will be slow, strenuous and protracted, as the change cannot be brought about easily. It has to be fought at emotional, cognitive and action levels. The struggle has to be carried on within caste, class, race, religion, everywhere in which manwoman relationships figure and matter.

Appendix-1

Women in Power and Decision-Making

Global commitments

This chapter of the *Platform for Action* focuses on achieving effective participation by women in decision-making in elected bodies, public administrative entities, political parties, the judiciary and civil society. The *Platform* sets out two strategic objectives.

- Take measures to ensure women's access to and full participation in power structures and decision-making.
- Increase women's capacity to participate in decision-making and leadership.

Two articles of the *Convention on the Elimination of All Forms of Discrimination against Women* (CEDAW) deal with women's participation in political and public life. Article 7 commits States parties to ensure equality between women and men in political and public life, including the right to vote, to be eligible for election, to participate in formulating government policy, to hold public office and to perform public functions. The Convention includes the right to participate in non-governmental organisations and other associations. Article 8 requires States parties to ensure that women have equal opportunities with men to represent their governments at the international level and to participate in the work of international organisations. The Committee on the Elimination of Discrimination against Women provided additional guidance in the implementation of the Convention in 1997 in its General Recommendation 23, which highlighted the application of the Convention to all levels of government and to the activities of a range of organisations concerned with public and political life, including public boards, local councils, and the activities of political parties, trade unions and professional associations. General Recommendation 23 also stated that: "It is the Government's fundamental responsibility to encourage these initiatives to lead and guide public opinion and change attitudes that discriminate against women or discourage women's involvement in political and public life."[1]

The Commission on the Status of Women continued to pay attention to the issue and adopted agreed conclusions on women and decision-making processes in 1997 and 2006.[2]

In its resolution 1325 (2000) on women, peace and security, the Security Council called on Member States to increase the representation of women in all institutions and mechanisms dealing with the prevention, management and resolution of conflict, including as special representatives and envoys of the Secretary-General and within the field operations as military observers, civilian police, human rights and humanitarian personnel.

The importance of the issue has been recognized within the framework of the Millennium. Development Goals. One of the indicators for monitoring Millennium Development Goal 3 on gender equality is the proportion of seats held by women in national parliaments.

The 2005 World Summit Outcome reaffirmed the commitments to increased representation of women in government decision-making bodies, including opportunities to participate fully in the political process.[3]

Progress at the national level

Marked progress has been made since 1995 in the numbers of women elected to national parliaments. The table below includes the 20 countries that achieved over 30 per cent representation of women in 2006, which compares favourably with the very short list of 5 countries that had achieved this in 1995 (Denmark, Finland, the Netherlands; Norway, Sweden).[4]

Rwanda achieved 48.8 per cent representation of women in the 2003 elections, a dramatic increase from the 17.1 per cent representation in 1995 that illustrated the positive results of focused and coordinated efforts to address this issue in the period of post-conflict reconstruction. Several other countries in the table are also post-conflict countries: Burundi, Mozambique, and South Africa. As noted by the Inter-Parliamentary Union, for countries in transition, "the process of establishing new constitutions and institutions and rewriting the rules of the political landscape provides a golden opportunity for women to influence the process and make their voices heard, especially in the drafting of electoral and political party laws."[5]

It is also notable that, in addition to the post-conflict group, there is one other country in Sub-Saharan Africa and another four in Central and South America that have passed the 30 per cent threshold and have considerably higher representation of women than a number of OECD countries with more resources and more established traditions of electoral politics, again demonstrating that the advancement of women is possible through political will and targeted action.

Almost all of the countries 20 countries included in the table have used some form of electoral quotas to ensure that women account for a certain number of percentage of candidates for office or officeholders, whether through a constitutional commitment, a provision of election

Women in national parliaments, 2006

Country	*%*	*Last*	*Electoral*	*If quota & type of quota women elections system*
Rwanda	48.8	2003	List PR	Yes - constitutional commitment, legislation establishing 30% reserved seats (indirectly elected)
Sweden	45.3	2002	List PR	Yes - voluntary party quotas for candidates
Costa Rica	38.6	2006	List PR	Yes - legislated quota of 40% women candidates on party lists
Norway	37.9	2005	List PR	Yes - voluntary party quotas for candidates
Finland	37.5	2003	List PR	No
Denmark	36.9	2005	List PR	No - but did have at times in the past
Netherlands	36.7	2003	List PR	Yes - voluntary party quotas for candidates
Cuba	36.0	2003	Majority*	No
Spain	36.0	2004	List PR	Yes - voluntary party quotas for candidates
Argentina	35.0	2005	List PR	Yes - constitutional commitment; legislated quota of 30% women on party lists; political party quotas for candidates
Mozambique	34.8	2004	List PR	Yes - voluntary party quotas for candidates

Belgium	34.7	2003	List PR	Yes - legislated quota of 33% women on party lists
Austria	33.9	2002	List PR	Yes - voluntary party quotas for candidates
Iceland	33.3	2003	List PR	Yes - voluntary party quotas for candidates
South Africa	32.8	2004	List PR	Yes - voluntary party quotas for candidates
New Zealand	32.2	2005	Mixed M & PR	No
Germany	31.8	2005	Mixed M & PR	Yes - voluntary party quotas for candidates
Guyana	30.8	2001	List PR	Yes - constitutional requirement for 33% quota for women on electoral lists
Burundi	30.5	2005	List PR	Yes - constitutional commitment, legislated quota of 30% women on party lists
Tanzania	30.4	2005	FPTP	Yes - constitutional quota, election law quota regulation (special seats)

PR= proportional representation; Mixed M & PR = combination of member and proportional representation; FPTP = first past the post; * in Cuba, the single nominated candidate must get the support of the majority of the electorate

Sources: IPU (2006). *Women in Politics: 60 years in retrospect; IPU* database on women in national parliaments; and IDEA International quota database

legislation, voluntary action by political parties, or some combination of these.[6]

Most countries have elected bodies at sub-national levels, some with state or provincial governments and most with elected local councils. Very little data is available for the intermediate (state or provincial level), but a database on women councillors and mayors is being developed by the organisation United Cities and Local Governments (UCLG) as part of their Global Programme on Women in Local Decision-Making. UCLG's conclusions from the preliminary and partial data available in 2005 were that 20 per cent of councillors overall were women and that the participation of women in local politics was increasing steadily.[7]

A number of countries have used constitutional or legislative quota systems to advance progress toward more equitable representation at the local level. The Global Database on Quotas for Women provides information on 30 countries with quotas at the sub-national level, mostly low and middle-income countries but also several in Europe - France, Greece, and Portugal.[8] In some countries, an initiative to decentralize decision-making to more local levels have provided an opportunity to establish measures to ensure the participation of women. For example, India led the way before the Fourth World Conference on Women in Beijing when its 1993 constitutional amendments to strengthen local governance included a measure to reserve one third of seats in *panchayats* (local governing councils) for women. Pakistan's Devolution of Power Plan of 2000 reserved one-third of seats for women at all sub-national levels.[9]

The Indian experience with reserved seats for women has been much studied, and it has been cited as indicating the way women's presence and participation can change politics:

> "In India studies of women in *panchayats* attest to the myriad ways women's presence has changed local politics. There are reports that women have made the *panchayats* more responsive

to community demands for infrastructure, housing, schools, and health. Women officials have improved implementation of various government programs, and their presence has made women citizens more likely to take advantage of state services and demand their rights. When women are the heads of *panchayats,* there is a greater likelihood that policies that are sensitive to women's needs will be implemented. Such effects take time to register, however. In the early stages of women's reservations, many women councilors seem merely to act as surrogates of their male relatives, but over time, they acquire the confidence and skills to act independently."[10]

Other notable developments include the election of women heads of government and state in Chile, Germany, and Liberia in 2005 and 2006, joining a number of other women presidents and prime ministers (Bangladesh, Finland, Ireland, Jamaica, Latvia, Mozambique, New Zealand, the Philippines, Republic of Korea, and Sao Tome and Principe).[11] However, this number of 13 women heads of government or state barely marks an increase compared to 1995.

Several countries reported increased representation of women in the judiciary or appointments of women to key judicial positions (including, for example, Chile, Djibouti, Egypt, Nicaragua, Slovenia, and Spain).[12] Four out of the nine judges on the Supreme Court of Canada, the country's final court of appeal, are women, including the Chief Justice. This is the result of considerable change throughout the Canadian judicial system in recent decades. In 2006, 29 per cent of all federally-appointed judges were women, compared to 0.05 per cent in 1969, the year that the Chief Justice began her career as a lawyer.[13]

Gaps and challenges

The developments noted above are promising and show what can be achieved. However, progress has been slow in all structures of power and types of decision-making.

Under-representation in national parliaments

Women accounted for 11.6 per cent on average of members of national parliaments in 1995, and this increased to only 17.3 per cent by May 2007 despite the target of 30 per cent that was to be reached by 1995 - a full decade earlier.[14] There remain a number of countries with no representation of women in parliament (including one that has not yet extended the vote to women).

Evidence suggests that a major factor influencing progress is the nature of electoral systems and the practices of political parties. Proportional representation systems result in a higher proportion of women than those with plurality/majority or mixed proportional systems: overall, the former have an average of 16 per cent women compared to 11 per cent for the latter based on data for 174 countries in 2003.[15] This is in large part because of the way the system interacts with the concerns and strategies *of* political parties: in plurality/majority systems the incentives to parties are to select the most "electable" candidate, whereas proportional systems allow for a greater number *of* candidates to be put forward. Even so, where women are placed on party lists also has a major influence on the likelihood of women obtaining a seat. Political parties thus play a key role in both types of system.

Even when elected, women are less likely than men to be in higher-level decision-making positions in national parliaments. The number of women serving as presiding officers in parliament decreased over the decade, down to 8% in 2005 from 10% in 1995.[16] They are also continue to be under-represented in cabinet appointments. While Sweden and Spain had achieved a gender balance in cabinet appointments in 2005, their performance is the exception rather than the rule - globally, the proportion was 14.3 per cent women as of January 2005.[17]

Numbers and effectiveness at the local level

Elections at the local level offer a greater number of opportunities for women simply because of the greater number of elected bodies and positions, and participation at the local level has served as a training ground for many politicians, both women and men. Great strides have been made through the use of quotas at the local level in several countries. For example, Bangladesh introduced reserved seats for women in local elections in 1997, which resulted in a total of 12,828 women elected to these reserved seats in some 4,400 locations, in addition to 110 women elected to general seats (of which there were over 39,000) and 20 women succeeding in the election as chairpersons (less than 1 per cent). However, it remains a challenge for these women to function effectively because their participation is not yet well-accepted by their male colleagues and they face considerable resistance in carrying out functions and exercising authority. Many of the women elected to office come with limited experience in elected office and government structures.[18] In Bangladesh and many other countries, the challenge of ensuring that local governments are effective and accountable to their citizens - both women and men - includes ensuring that male members have the capacity to work effectively with their female colleagues, and that the women members have the knowledge and skills to use the relevant procedures and address local issues. The trend toward decentralization of responsibilities to the local level increases the importance of addressing this challenge.

Women's share in public and private sector managerial positions

Women's representation in decision-making positions in the civil service and public sector bodies are also concerns of the Platform for Action. The limited information available to assess progress illustrates the challenges in this area. The European Commission's database on women and men in decision-making is one of the few sources that focusses specifically on senior public service positions. Considering the proportion of women in the highest-ranked civil service position under the Minister, only 5 of 31 countries passed the 30 per cent threshold in 2006, although several others achieved this at the second highest level.[19] Occupation data from labour force surveys on the census provides another source of data, although data about the public sector may be difficult to extract as labour force surveys generally combine information from the public and private sectors. The ILO has calculated that women's overall share of public and private sector managerial jobs (including posts as legislators, senior officials and managers) was between 20 and 40 percent in 48 of the 63 countries for which data could be obtained, a figure that remains considerably lower than women's overall share in employment.[20]

Finally, considering the participation of women in strategic decision-making in the private sector, the "glass ceiling" - the barriers that limit the numbers of women reaching the top of the corporate hierarchy - is still evident. In the United States, a 2005 survey of women corporate officers found that Fortune 500 companies had on average 21.8 corporate officers, *of* which women held on average 3.6 positions. The study found that there had been little change over the previous decade and concluded that, with this rate of progress, "it could take 40 years for women to achieve parity with men in corporate officer positions."[21] Another study by the same organisation found that the Fortune 500 companies with the highest percentages of women corporate officers, yielded higher returns than those with lower percentages of women.[22] In Europe, a 2006 study found that among Europe's top corporations, the number with at least one woman on their board was higher in 2006 than in 2004, but that European corporations were lagging behind their American counterparts, except in Scandinavia, where proactive policies had been taken. The study also found that few of the women on boards held leadership position - less than 2 percent held positions as chair of the board or chief executive officer.[23]

Norway responds to the lack of gender balance on corporate boards

Norway has been known as a leader on gender equality and in the participation of women in decision-making: women constitute almost 40 per cent of parliamentarians and women have held positions such as those of prime minister, supreme court justice and minister of defence. However, progress in the corporate sector has been much slower: in 2003, only 7 per cent of corporate board and executive positions were held by women. For state-owned companies, legislation passed in February 2002 requires at least 40 per cent representation of each sex on their boards by March 2003. The private sector was put on notice that they were expected to meet similar targets and was given two years to demonstrate compliance. By July 2005, only 68 of 519 companies had fulfilled the requirements, and while the percentage of women on boards had increased to 16 per cent, this was still far from the 40 per cent target. Legislation addressed to the private sector was therefore passed, effective in January 2006. The legislation requires existing companies to comply within two years and new companies to comply in order to be registered.

Sources: www.norwav.org/news/archive/2003/200303gender.htm; odin.dep.no/bid/english/news/speeches/004021-070005/dok-bn.html

Strategies to accelerate implementation

In addition to setting out government commitments the *Platform for Action* urges a range of actors to take measures in support of women's participation in power structures and decision-making. These include political parties, the private sector, trade unions, the judiciary, employers' organisations, academic institutions and civil society, among others. However, governments have a lead role in encouraging and facilitating action by others, as well as in implementing measures in the management of public sector institutions. National governments can:

- consider the potential for temporary special measures to accelerate progress toward gender balance in elected office, particularly in the context of electoral reform and decentralization;

- develop or support programmes that provide training to women candidates in the skills needed for effective campaigning, and to elected women in the skills in effectively carrying out their functions and supporting equality objectives;
- facilitate linkages among various actors seeking to bring gender equality issues and women's views into the decision-making process;
- establish specific time-bound targets and action plans for increasing women's representation in decision-making in the public sector;
- establish mechanisms to facilitate consideration of women candidates in appointments to senior positions in government and public sector boards and agencies;
- promote awareness and support for the goal of gender equality among decision-makers through public awareness campaigns; and
- strengthen monitoring, reporting and knowledge about women's participation in decisionmaking through improved data collection, dissemination and analysis.

Aspects of several of these strategies are discussed further in the text and boxes below.

Influencing the electoral process

Electoral quotas have been an important element in achieving progress in many countries, at both the national and local levels. However, quotas are only effective if they are appropriate to the particular electoral system of a country (or the level of government to which they apply). Proportional representation systems offer a broader range of options for quotas than plurality/majority systems. Even so, a quota initiative may require constitutional change or sanction, and the opportunity to introduce a quota system would therefore only arrive in the context of larger reform processes in which broad public support for them has been mobilized - as has been the case in a number of post-conflict countries. Quotas can be useful measures, but the design and implementation must be strategically pursued.

If quotas are intended to be implemented by political parties, they must be designed so that evasion is difficult. However, as voluntary implementation is preferable to implementation under compulsion, it would seem desirable to seek to build broad public support at the stage of formulating such provisions in order to facilitate implementation. Quotas can also have a downside if the nature of the quota-based system results in women members who are seen as having less legitimacy as elected representatives than their male peers. Political parties play a key role in the electoral system. Some observers have suggested that not only are they the gatekeepers in women's access to politics, but that quotas have been most successful when they have been adopted on a voluntary basis by political parties who come to see this as being in their own interest.[24]

Quota systems also need to be supplemented with other policies to enable women to be effective representatives. The importance of access to training and skills development was emphasised by the United Nations Expert Group on Equal Participation of Women and Men in Decision-making Processes:

> "Given that many women have had little experience with running for political office, it is of utmost importance that training be made readily available to allow women to develop and fine-tune their political skills. Once in office, women may also benefit from leadership training and mentoring to increase efficiency and ensure sustainability.
>
> Training programmes should also target men, to expose them to the complexities of gender discrimination and the necessity of and mechanisms for promoting women in public office."[25]

Conditions for the effectiveness of quotas in enhancing women's voice in political bodies

The UN Millenium Project's Task Force report, *Taking Action: Achieving Gender Equality and Empowering Women*, provides a good summary of four major lessons of experience about the effectiveness of quotas.

- **"A country's electoral system strongly influences the impact of quotas.** Quotas work best in closedlist, proportional representation systems with placement mandates and where electoral districts are large - where many candidates are elected from each electoral district and parties can expect several candidates running in the district to gain a seat...."
- **"Placement mandates are critical to the success of quotas in closed list proportional representation electoral systems.** Because candidates are elected from party lists in the order in which they appear, placement on the list determines the chances of being elected. Placement mandates require parties to place women in high or "electable" positions on party lists (for example, by alternations of women's positions with men's on the party list). This system sets up a reasonably direct relationship between the number of women candidates and the number of women elected...."
- **"Quota laws must specify details of implementation.** Vague laws leave too much discretion to political parties to apply - or fail to apply - quotas as they see fit. ... "
- **"For quota laws to be effective, there must be sanctions for non-compliance.** The strongest sanction is to have a party's list of candidates declared invalid and for the party to be forbidden from contesting the election. For these sanctions to work, judges must be able to monitor party compliance and groups must be able to challenge non-compliant lists in court...."

Source: UN Millennium Project (2005). *Taking Action.*

Facilitating linkages among elected women

Women elected to parliament at the national or local level remain in a minority, and many are relative newcomers to the process, so alliances among them and with other women's and equality advocates can be important to enabling women to be effective as parliamentarians and in advocacy for equality issues. The national women's machinery can play a role in facilitating the formation and work of such alliances. In Rwanda, for example, seminars during the constitutional process brought together the Forum of Women Parliamentarians, the Legal and Constitutional Committee, the Ministry of Gender Issues and representatives of civil society organisations. Through close collaboration among these actors, progress was made in a number of areas: mobilization of women to participate in the constitutional drafting and in the elections as voters and candidates; sensitization of the public on existing inequalities and women's rights; sensitization of decision-makers and planners on gender equality issues; development of a national gender equality policy; and joint work to review and advocate the repeal of discriminatory legislation.[27]

In Uganda, a non-partisan Women's Caucus brought together members of the Constituent Assembly elected in 1994 and, with the assistance of the national women's machinery, organized seminars and skills-training workshops on advocacy, campaign management, constituency building, parliamentary procedures, etc. They also formed links with key organisations such as the Uganda Women Lawyers' Association, which assisted with the consideration of constitutional provisions, as well as with organisations that enabled the Women's Caucus to remain informed of the views of women at the grass-roots and to communicate with them. The experience gained through their effective interventions during the Constituent Assembly formed the basis for later work in building the capacity of women leaders at the local level and potential candidates for parliament, and in incorporating gender equality perspectives in legislation before parliament.[28]

Many countries have established formal parliamentary bodies to consider issues related to the position of women and gender equality. These take a range of forms and many include men as well as women. An informative on-line database on the structures and mandates of such specialized bodies is maintained by the Inter-Parliamentary Union. It includes, for example: the Gender Caucus in Burkina Faso, the Network of Parliamentarians on Gender Issues in Niger, the Standing Committee on the Status of Women in Canada, and the Special Committee on Gender and Equality in Uruguay.[29] These bodies provide forums for the discussion of gender equality issues among members and potentially a forum for exchanges with civil society organisations and advocates. This can be an important opportunity for another form of participation by women in decision-making by providing opportunities for women's organisations to participate in discussions of policy decisions that shape their societies and affect their lives. This is another area in which national women's machineries can play facilitating roles through, for example, bringing women's organisations to the attention of the parliamentary bodies, or enabling women's organisations to develop advocacy skills.

Supporting women candidates through training, media campaigns, and guidance - Vietnam

In Vietnam, the representation of women in national parliament has increased from 18.5 per cent in the 1992 elections to 26.2 per cent in 1997 and 27.4 per cent in 2002; in 2004 Vietnam had the highest representation of women in parliament in Asia. Progress has been supported by initiatives of the National Committee for the Advancement of Women (NCFAW, the inter-ministerial committee that is Vietnam's national machinery for women's advancement). For the 1997 elections, leadership training sessions were held in six locations for 144 women candidates. The training focused on campaigning and presentation skills, and on concrete strategies to increase chances of success. For the subsequent elections, 216 women candidates benefited from the leadership training.

For the People's Council Elections at the sub-national level (provincial, district and commune), the NCFAW and the Vietnam Women's Union (VWU) organised training courses on leadership skills for almost 18,000 women candidates in preparation for the 1999 elections, with further sessions held for the 2004 elections. There was also a media campaign to promote positive images of women in leadership and encourage the public to vote for women. Further support to the candidates is provided by the "Manual for Women in People's Councils" developed by the VWU. The manual focuses on women in leadership, the roles and functions of Peoples Councils, necessary skills and a better understanding of gender equality issues.

Source: National Report of Vietnam (2004)

Engaging journalists in discussions on gender equality to increase coverage and public debate

In Southern Africa, a set of training workshops targeting media practitioners and women in or seeking public office were held in advance of the elections anticipated in 2004 and 2005 in seven countries in Southern Africa. The workshops were planned and led by Gender Links, an organisation that promotes gender equality in and through media, as part of its gender, media and governance programme. The workshops had a number of aims including an increase in the gender awareness and skill of media practitioners, building relationships between women in politics and media decision-makers and practitioners, empowering women with practical skills for dealing with the media, and assisting the media in thinking through the gender dimensions of election. coverage.

Subsequent monitoring showed a substantial increase in the quantity and quality pf coverage of gender issues linked to the elections in the media organisations reached through the newsroom-based training that was part of the training in each country.

- South Africa: gender was a key point of analysis of the election, especially in the announcement of the new cabinet; monitoring also showed an increase in reports drawing on women as sources of news from 13 per cent in 1999 to 26 per cent in 2004;
- Malawi: newspapers and radio stations made a special effort to feature women candidates and to comment on women's under-representation;
- Botswana: the media raised an outcry when election results showed a decline in women's representation, which had a clear result on the announcement of nominated MPs and the new cabinet.
- Mauritius: when the ruling party boycotted a "women in politics" seminar after having faced tough questions on these issues, the media took the government to task for failing to deliver on its gender equality promises.

The workshops also resulted in links between gender equality activists, media and women politicians and thus established a foundation for ongoing dialogue and the development of news stories.

The various approaches followed and the lessons learned for future training are well documented and the initiative resulted in a rich set of resources that are available on-line. For an overview and country-specific reports, see: www.genderlinks.ora.zalitem.php?i id=64; for the resources generated and further developments with work on the "gender, media and elections" theme, see: www.genderlinks.org.zalpage.php?p id=118.

Making information on qualified women more accessible to decision-makers

Ensuring that decision-makers have ready access to information about potential women candidates for senior appointments is a way of counter-balancing the more established networks that men with similar experience may have to bring their name to the attention of decisionmakers. It is also a practical way to respond to the tendency of managers to assume that qualified candidates will have qualities similar to their own, or that there are no qualified women in the field - assumptions that work against women as long as they are a small minority in decisionmaking positions.

The development of a directory or database of women in leadership positions is an approach reported by a number of countries. A more active approach has been taken by New Zealand, which has established an office that provides a service both to government decisionmakers seeking to identify potential candidates and to women with the relevant interests and skills (see box). This approach thus also addresses the information constraint often faced by women - that appointments to senior positions may be made before information about the openings reaches women who may be qualified and interested.

Sector-specific strategies may also deliver good results. For example, women who could be qualified for appointments to the judiciary may also be less known to decision-makers than similarly qualified men. An approach taken by Canada to broaden the field of candidates for judicial appointments was to shift from a top-down selection system to one in which those interested in an appointment are required to submit an application, which is then reviewed by committees composed of judges, lawyers and citizens. The committees determine whether the candidates are qualified before the names enter a pool for possible appointments. This has brought into the system many women who may have been unnoticed in a strictly top-down system.[32]

In the Philippines, the Civil Service Commission revised a range of policies in support of the target of gender balance in executive positions

The Government of the Philippines has taken a number of steps to increase the number of women at the decision-making level of the civil service. The Civil Service Commission (CSC) issued a Memorandum Circular in 1999 setting a target of 50-50 representation of women and men in executive positions and requiring regular reporting by sex on nominations, appointments and positions held. In order to advance progress in meeting the target, the CSC (in collaboration with the National Commission on the Role of Filipino Women (NCRFW) and the Career Executive Service Board) has undertaken three programmes to increase women's capacity and skills.

1) Career Advancement of Women in Government Services (CAPWINGS) seeks to enhance support mechanisms, capacity building, training and other enabling mechanisms for women employees. The programme has worked on improving working conditions, preventing sexual harassment in the workplace, facilitating career advancement and advocacy. Policies enacted include: paternity leave, leaves for various family-related occasions, establishment of day care centres, flexible working arrangements (including modified maternity leave, part-time work and flexible hours).
2) Merit Promotion Plan, which guides promotions based on merit, and has been revised to ensure that gender biases do not obstruct recruitment and promotion and to emphasize equal opportunities for women and men;
3) Directory of Women on the Move, which provides information about qualified women candidates for vacancies in the Cabinet and other executive positions to ensure that appointing authorities have information and choices about qualified women for top posts.

Source: Philippines periodic report to CEDAW (2004).

"Nominations Service" to support the gender balance target for statutory bodies - New Zealand

The government of New Zealand's target for 2010 is to have equal representation of women and men in the members of government statutory bodies. To achieve this, the Ministry of Women's Affairs has established the Nominations Service, a unit with 3 staff and a budget, which focuses on identifying women with appropriate experience and ensuring these women are known to decision-makers. A stock-taking in 2004 showed that significant progress had been made: 41 per cent of the directors and committee members were women (of 397 statutory bodies with a total of 2,605 members), compared to about 25 per cent in 1993. However, there continued to be differences among sectors, with higher representation of women in social development, health and related fields, and lower numbers in sectors such as agriculture, economic development and transport. The Nominations Service was able to learn from experience and to adjust strategies so that its advice and services are now sought after. This required that it develop a strong reputation among both decision-makers and candidates for the database. It has therefore developed "a rigorous `recruitment agency' competency matching approach," providing the links between those needing skills and those with skills, and has a proactive communication strategy with potential nominees and database members (including a website that provides further information on its procedures: www.mwa.govt. nz/women-on-boards).

Sources: Panel presentation on "Women in Decision-Making at all Levels," Commonwealth Meetings on the eve of the 2006 session of the Commission on the Status of Women.

Strengthening data and analysis of issues and progress

There continues to be a need for better data to assess issues and progress. Data are lacking on many aspects of women's participation in leadership and decision-making positions. A United Nations review of data collection at the national level found that statistical agencies in many countries do not routinely collect and disseminate statistics on women in power and decision-making, due to a lack of capacity for collection and reporting and poorly developed methodologies for the use of existing data to examine gender equality issues in this area.[35]

The best tracked level is the most clearly defined and visible - the number of women in national parliaments and key elected offices. The work of the Inter-Parliamentary Union has served to ensure reporting on these figures by national parliaments and the presentation of this information in an international database.[36] Efforts are also being made by the organisation United Cities and Local

Governments (UCLG), which has begun work on a database on women's participation in municipal and local governments, 17 but this is a more complicated task because of the greater number and variety of levels and because limited data on these levels is gathered by national agencies.

Equally important is improved data on women's participation in other types of decisionmaking positions in the public sector, such as senior positions in the public service appointments to the judiciary, and positions on the boards of public agencies. Data on the proportion of women in managerial jobs in the public and private sectors together is not sufficiently specific to monitor the implementation of government commitments to the increased participation of women in decision-making positions over which the government itself has the power of promotion or appointment. Better data on women in such positions at the sub-national level is also important to the elaboration of policies at that level, and is particular urgent in those countries in which decentralization processes increase the scope of responsibilities of local governments in policy development and service delivery.

Resources

Websites

- IDEA (International Institute for Democracy and Electoral Assistance) gender equality website: www.idea.int/gender/. Website with discussions of issues and developments as well further resources on specific issues See in particular the document by IDEA and Stockholm University, *Women in Parliament: Beyond Numbers Handbook* (updated 2005), which reviews obstacles faced by women entering parliament, possible solutions, and influence strategies fore those elected, and presents informative case studies in all these areas: www.idea.int/publications/wip2/index.cfm. Also see this organisation's work on a *Global database on quotas for women:* information and analysis on the various types of quotas in use in different countries, as well as country-specific information: www.quotaproject.ory/ (all accessed 28 June 2007).

- The Inter-Parliamentary Union (IPU) has several sites on women's political participation: regularly updated data on women in national parliaments: www.ipu.org/win-e/world.htm; a database on specialized parliamentary bodies dealing with the status of women and gender equality, with information about the date of creation, mandate, subjects dealt with, working methods, relations with other bodies, etc. www.ipu.org/parline-e/Instanceadvanced.asp; and a searchable bibliographical database on various aspects of political participation by women: www.ipu.org/bdf-e/BDFsearch.asp (all accessed 28 June 2007).
- iKNOW Politics Network (International network on Women and Politics) is "an on-line workspace designed to serve the needs of elected officials, candidates, political party leaders and members, researchers, students and practitioners interested in advancing women in politics." It is a joint initiative of several organisations including IPU and IDEA and provides access to resources and expertise and opportunities to share experiences. www.iknowpolitics.org (accessed 28 June 2007).

Reports and tools

- Inter-Parliamentary Union, *Women in politics: 60 years in retrospect* (2006), a set of 6 "datasheets", including comparisons between 1995 and 2006 (datasheet 2); a chronology of women heads of state or government since 1945 (datasheet 4). an overview of data on women in parliament in the same period (datasheet 5), and a paper on "the participation of women and men in decision-making: the parliamentary dimension" (datasheet 6). www.ipu.org /PDF/publications/wmninfolit06_en.pdf (accessed 28 June 2007)

- United Nations, Department of Political Affairs (2005). *Women and Elections. Guide on promoting the participation of women in elections.* Handbook intended to provide a quick reference guide to assist those working to promote greater participation of women in electoral processes in post-conflict countries, inspired by an Expert Group meeting on the same theme. www.un.org/womenwatch/osagi/was/womenandelections.html (accessed 28 June 2007).
- United Nations, Division for the Advancement of Women (2005). Expert Group Meeting on "Equal participation of women and men in decision-making processes, with particular emphasis on political participation and leadership." Papers by experts, as well as the back ground paper and the final report are available at: www.un.orglwomenwatch/daw/egm/eql-men/documents_ preview.html (accessed 27 June 2007).
- UNRISD, *Gender Equality: Striving for Justice in an Unequal World (2005)* has a major section on women in politics and public life, with discussions on women's participation in electoral systems, women's efforts to reshape politics, gender and good governance, and the implication of decentralization. www.unrisd.org/ (search by title) (accessed 27 June 2007).
- Woodward, Alison (2001). *Going for Gender Balance: a guide for balanced decisionmaking. Good practices to achieve gender-balanced representation in political and social decision-making.* Division for Equality between Women and Men. Council of Europe, EG-S*BP (2001)1.* Provides a concise overview of issues and brief case studies of promising initiatives (in European member states) in various arenas of decision-making political parties, public administration, trade unions, women's organisations), www.humanrights.coe.int/equality/Eng/WordDocs/Document%20list. htm (under women in politics and decision-making) (accessed *27* June *2007).*
- Vinnicombe, Susan et. al. *Making Good Connections: Best Practice for Women's Corporate Networks.* Report on how to set up and run women's networks. Developed

under the auspices of the Cranfield Centre for Developing Women leaders. www.som.cranfield.ac.uk/som/research/centres/edwbl~'downloads/contiections.pdf (accessed 27 June 2007).

Notes

1. CEDAW General Recommendation No. 23 (16th session, 1997), para. 28: www.un.org/womenwatch;'daw/cedaw/recommendations/recomm.htm#recom23 (accessed 28 June 2007).
2. CSW agreed conclusions: www.un.org/womenwatch/daw/esw/ (select session., the agreed conclusions) (accessed 26 June 2007).
3. *2005 World Summit Outcome,* United Nations General Assembly Resolution A/RES/60/ 1, para. 58. www.un.org/summit2005/documents.html (accessed 29 June 2007).
4. Inter-Parliamentary Union (2006). *Women in politics: 60 years in retrospect,* Data Sheet 2. www.ipu.or /PDF/publications/wmninfokit06 en.pdf (accessed 28 June 2007).
5. Inter-Parliamentary Union (2006). *Women in politics: 60 years in retrospect,* Data Sheet 6, p.4 www.ipu.org PDF/publications/wmninfokitO6sen.pdf (accessed 28 Jwie 2007).
6. On types of quotas, see the *Global Database on Quotas for Women: www.quotaproJect.org / index.cfm* (accessed 28 June 2007).
7. UCLG: www.cities-localgovemments.or /ucla/ (see gender statistics) (accessed 28 June 2007).
8. *Global Database on Quotas for Women: www.quotaproject.org / system.efrn*#constlocal (accessed 28 June 2007).
9. UN *Millennium* Project (2005). *Taking Action: achieving gender equality and empowering women.* Task Force on Education and Gender Equality, p.105. www.unmillenniumproject.org/reports/tf gender.htm (accessed 26 June 2007).
10. UN *Millennium* Project (2005). *Taking Action: achieving gender equality and empowering women.* Task Force on Education and Gender Equality, pp.105-106. www.unmillenniumproicct.org/reports/tf_gendenhtm (accessed 26 June 2007).
11. See Worldwide Guide to Women in Leadership: www.guide2womenleaders.com/ (accessed 28 June 2007).

12. United Nations (2005). *Review of the Implementation of the Beijing Piatform for Action and the outcome documents of the .special session of the General Assembly entitled "Women 2000: gender equality, development and peace for the twenty-first century. " Report of the Secretary-General.* E/CN.6/2005/2, para. 334.
13. McLachlin, Beverly (Chief Justice of Canada) (2006). "Why we need women judges," Speech to the International Association of Women Judges, 8th Biennial Conference, Sydney, Australia, May 2006: www.iawi.orQ/what/sydney.asp (accessed 28 June 2007).
14. Data for 1995 from Inter-Parliamentary Union (2006). *Women in politics: 60 years in retrospect,* Data Sheet 5. wwnv.ipu.org/ PDF/publications/wmninfoki-06 en.pdf, data for 2007 from the IPU database on women in national parliaments www.ipu.org/ wmn-e/world.htm (accessed 28 June 2007); the 30% target for 1995 was set by ECOSOC in 1990 and is referred to in the *Platform for Action,* para. 182.
15. UNRISD (2005). *Gender Equality: Striving for Justice in an Unequal World,* p 152, 2003 data for 174 countries: www.unrisd.org/ (search by title) (accessed 27 June 2007).
16. Inter-Parliamentary Union (2006). *Women in politics: 60 years in retrospect,* Data Sheet 6, p.6 (both women ministers and presiding officers). www.i_pu.org,/PDF/publications/ 'wmtuinfokitO6 en.Llf (accessed 28 June 2007).
17. Inter-Parliamentary Union (2006). *Women in politics: 60 years in retrospect,* Data Sheet 6, p.6 (both women ministers and presiding officers). www.ipu.orb/PDF%publications,' WmiiinfokitO6_en.pd (accessed 28 June 2007).
18. South Asia Partnership Bangladesh, "Capacity profile of Union Parishad elected women member," study-funded by CIDA's PLAGE project in collaboration with the Ministry of Women and Children Affairs, n.d.
19. European Commission, Database on women and men in decision-making (data last updated 04-12-06): ec.europa.cu/ employment social/women men stats/out/measures out55 en.htm (accessed 28 June 2007).
20. ILO (2004). *Breaking through the glass ceiling: women in management. www.ilo.org/dyn/gender/does/RES./292/ f267981337* (accessed 28 June 2007).

21. Catalyst (2006). 2005 *Census of Corporate Officers and Top Earners for the Fortune 500.*, p.9. www.catal sy t org/ knowledgeititles/title.php?pace=cen WOTE02 (accessed 28 June 2007).
22. Catalyst (2004). *The Bottom Line: Connecting Corporate Performance and Gender Diversity: www.^atalyst.org / knowledge / titles / title.php?page=lead* finperf 04 (accessed 28 June 2007).
23. European Professional Women's Network, *Second Bi-annual EuropeanPWNBoardWomen Monitor 2006. www.europeanpwn.net / files / boardwomen* resent large120606.pdf (accessed 28 June 2007).
24. For example, see chapter 9 in UNRISD (2005). *Gender Equality: Striving for Justice in an Unequal World. www.unrisd.org / (search* by title) (accessed 27 June 2007).
25. United Nations, Division for the Advancement of Women (2005). *Report of the Expert Group Meeting on Equal participation ofwomen and men in decision-making processes, with particular emphasis on political participation and leadership."* EGM/EPDM/2005/REPORT, para. 58. www.un.org/womenwaich/daw/egm/egl-men/FinalReport. pdf (accessed 3 July 2007).
26. *UN Millennium* Project (2005). *Taking Action: kchieving gender equality and empowering women.* Task Force on Education and Gender Equality, pp. 108-109. www.unmillenniumproject. org/reeports,,tf ender.htm (accessed 26 June 2007).
27. Kantengwa, Juliana (2004). "Women's participation in electoral processes in post conflict countries: the case of Rwanda", Paper for panel discussion at the United Nations (March 2004): www.un.org/womenwatch/osagi/meetings/2004/CSW48Panel/ CSW4SPaiie!.htm ; Kareen Jabre (2004). "Enhancing the role of women in electoral processes in post-conflict countries: post election support, " paper for Expert Group Meeting, United Nations, (January 2004): www.un.org/womenwatch/osagi/ meetings/2004/EGMclectoral/index.htnil (both sites accessed 28 June 2007).
28. Mukibi, Benigna (2000). "Alliances for gender and politics: the Uganda Women's Caucus," in UNDP, *Women :s Political Participation and Good Governance:* 21" *Century Challenges.*

www.undp.org / governance / docs / Gender-Pub-21 stcentury pdf (accessed 27 June 2007).

29. IPU database on specialized parliamentary bodies dealing with the status of women and gender equality: www.ipu.org/parliiie-e/instanceadvanced.asp (accessed 28 June 2007).
30. Vietnam (2004). National report for the ten-year review and appraisal of the implementation of the *Beijing Declaration and Pla J6rm f6r Action: www.tin.org / womenwatch / daw, / Review / en* Ig ish/responses.litm (accessed 27 June 2007).
31. Referenced websites accessed 28 June 2007.
32. McLachlin, Beverly (Chief Justice of Canada) (2006). "Why we need women judges," Speech to the International Association of Women Judges, 8`h Biennial Conference, Sydney, Australia, (May 2006): www.iawi.org/what/sydney.asp (accessed 28 June 2007).
33. Philippines periodic report to CEDAW (2004), para. 39, 250, 252. www.un-or7/womenwatch/daw/cedaw/36sess.htin (accessed 28 June 2007). For updated information about initiatives of the civil Serivce Commission, see their gender equality website: www.csc.gov.ph/GAD/index.htmi (accessed 28 June 2007).
34. *Report of the Commonwealth Meetings on the eve of the 50th Session of the UN Commission* on *the Status q /* Women, 25-26 February 2006, New York, presentation by New Zealand in Annex B-VII: www.thecommonwealth.org/document/ 152447!report_of the commonwealth meetings on the eve ofhtm (accessed 28 June 2007). (New Zealand website referred to in box also accessed 28 June 2007.)
35. United Nations, Statistics Division (2006). *The World's Women 2005: Progress in Statistics, p.81. unstats.un.org / unsddemographic / productsiindwm / wwpub.htm* (accessed 26 June 2007).
36. Inter-Parliamentary Union database on women in national parliaments: www.ipu.org/wrnn-e/world.htm (accessed 28 June 2007).
37. UCLG: www.cities-localgovemments.org/uclg/ see gender statistics (accessed 28 June 2007).